GW00838574

THE MEANI
INTERNATIONA   ...ON

Edwin O. Reischauer (1910–1990) was born and raised in Japan. He earned his Ph.D. from Harvard University and went on to teach there for decades. He served as the American Ambassador to Japan in the 1960s and was the author of numerous books on the history, culture, and people of Japan, including *The Japanese Today: Change and Continuity* and *Japan: The Story of a Nation*. In 1985, the John Hopkins University School of Advanced International Studies opened the Reischauer Center for East Asian Studies, named in his honor.

THE MEANING OF INTERNATIONALIZATION

PRACTICAL ADVICE FOR A CONNECTED PLANET

真の国際化とは

by Edwin O. Reischauer
エドウィン・O・ライシャワー

Bilingual Edition
Translated by Masao Kunihiro
國弘正雄 訳

TUTTLE PUBLISHING
Tokyo • Rutland, Vermont • Singapore

Published by Tuttle Publishing, an imprint of Periplus Editions (HK) Ltd., with editorial offices at 364 Innovation Drive, North Clarendon, Vermont 05759 USA and 61 Tai Seng Avenue, #02-12, Singapore 534167

Library of Congress Cataloging-in-Publication Data

Reischauer, Edwin O. (Edwin Oldfather), 1910-1990
  The meaning of internationalization / Edwin O. Reischauer.
    p. cm.
  ISBN 978-4-8053-1034-2 (pbk.)
1. Japan--Relations--Foreign countries. 2. Internationalism. I. Title.
  DS845.R44 2009
  303.48'252--dc22

                            2008033111

ISBN 978-4-8053-1034-2

Distributed by

North America, Latin America & Europe
Tuttle Publishing
364 Innovation Drive
North Clarendon, VT 05759-9436 U.S.A.
Tel: 1 (802) 773-8930; Fax: 1 (802) 773-6993
info@tuttlepublishing.com
www.tuttlepublishing.com

Japan
Tuttle Publishing
Yaekari Building, 3rd Floor 5-4-12 Osaki
Shinagawa-ku, Tokyo 141 0032
Tel: (81) 03 5437-0171; Fax: (81) 03 5437-0755
tuttle-sales@gol.com

Asia Pacific
Berkeley Books Pte. Ltd.
61 Tai Seng Avenue, #02-12
Singapore 534167
Tel: (65) 6280-1330; Fax: (65) 6280-6290
inquiries@periplus.com.sg
www.periplus.com

11   10 09   10 9 8 7 6 5 4 3 2 1

Printed in Singapore

CONTENTS

FOREWORD

In Japan in recent years, "international" and "internationalization" have become very popular vogue words. In contemporary American slang one might call them buzzwords. But unfortunately such terms often come to mean very different things to different people. For example, in French politics in the past, "radical" came virtually to mean "conservative." Many countries today like to call themselves "democratic republics," even though in any real democracy they would seem to be almost the opposite.

In the West "international" has always stood in contrast to "national." It suggests understanding and cooperation between different lands rather than isolation and narrow self-interest. It gives promise of peace among countries and harmony based on international law and institutions. Nationalism, on the contrary, implies military conflict and economic warfare resulting from clashes of national interest. Some people do fear that internationalism will weaken or corrupt their lands, but the term on the whole is overwhelmingly favorable.

序　文

　「国際的」とか「国際化」ということばが昨今の日本では流行語としてよく使われるようになりました。いまのアメリカの俗語でいうなら、はやりことば（バズワード）、とでもいうのでしょうか。でもこのようなことばは不幸なことに、しばしば人によってうんと違った内容を意味するようになっています。かつてのフランスの政治においては、「過激な（ラジカル）」ということばが、事実上、「保守的な（コンサーバティブ）」を意味するように変わっていったことなどはその一例です。また今日、真の民主主義政体とはほとんど正反対であるにもかかわらず、「民主主義共和国」と自国を呼びたがっている国もたくさんあります。

　欧米における international ということばは、national ということばとずっと好対照をなしてきました。孤立や狭い意味での自己利益のかわりに、異なる国同士が理解し協力しあっていくことを示唆することばです。また国際法や国際的な機構をもとに、国家間の平和や調和を約束するというひびきももっています。それに反しナショナリズムは、国家利益のぶつかりあいがもとで、軍事的な対立や経済的な争い、という含みをもちます。インターナショナリズムは、自分たちの国を弱体化し堕落させるだけだと怖れている人々もおりますが、このことばは総じてよい意味を伝えます。

Internationalization clearly has a basically good meaning in Japan as well, or else it would not be so popular. But negative attitudes toward the term are much stronger than in the West. Some Japanese equate internationalization with Westernization and fear that it would bring a further loss of the uniqueness they claim for Japan. Such attitudes, however, are quite mistaken. The rapid changes that undoubtedly are taking place in Japan are the product of the development of science and technology and the resultant prosperity they have brought to Japan, not the unwanted results of internationalization. How many Japanese would wish to forego their present affluence and worldwide economic leadership to return to impoverished isolation?

Some Japanese also contrast the international turmoil of the contemporary world with the strict peace and order of Tokugawa times, forgetting the harsh personal suppression that accompanied this earlier system. They compare the long peace which Tokugawa isolation made possible with the wars that swept the rest of the world. To them international contacts are associated with war and the frightening threat of imperialist domination of the past. Peace and tranquility seem more attainable through the avoidance of

　国際化ということばは日本でも基本的によい意味をもっていることははっきりしています。さもなければ、これほど人気があろうはずはないからです。でも、このことばに対する否定的な考え方は、欧米におけるよりもぐんと強いのです。日本人の中には、国際化を欧米化と同じものだと考え、日本のもっている独自性——と彼らが主張してやまないもの——をいま以上に損なうものである、と怖れている向きがあります。しかし、この手の考え方は完全にまちがっています。日本でいま急激に起きている変化は、科学技術が進歩し、その結果、日本にもたらされた繁栄の結果なのでして、国際化の望みもしない結果ではないのです。今日の繁栄や経済面での世界的な主導権を手放して、かつての貧しい孤立に戻りたいと望んでいる日本人など、いったいどれくらいいるでしょうか。

　また日本人の中には混乱にみちた今日世界を、あくまでも平和や秩序が保たれた徳川時代と比較する向きもありますが、彼らはそれがどれほど苛酷な個人次元での抑圧をともなう制度であったかを、とんと忘れています。徳川期の孤立が可能にした長期にわたる平和を、日本以外を吹き荒れた戦乱と比較しているのです。彼らにとって、国際的なかかわりとは、戦争や過去の帝国主義的な支配のもたらす恐るべき脅威と結びついているのです。できるだけ国際的なかかわりを避けることが、平和や安寧を手に入れるゆえんであると思っているのです。それだけにこれらの人々にとって国際化などは、い

international contacts in so far as possible. Internationalization to such people, therefore, is a dubious and slightly repellent term. But they are grossly mistaken in these concepts. Japan is like a creature that has become much too large for its old protective shell of isolation. Unable under modern conditions to grow a new and bigger shell, it must devise new means to protect itself. Internationalization is obviously the only means Japan has to continue its prosperity and survive in peace.

Internationalization thus is a key word for Japan today. People should know its true meaning and also its implications and problems. Without it, Japan cannot continue its present affluence and world leadership as an economic giant. It cannot even survive. It is for this reason that I have composed this little essay on the meaning of internationalization to Japan and some of the problems Japanese need to consider when thinking about it.

Edwin O. Reischauer
March 13, 1988

かがわしくもあり、うとましくもあることばなのです。でも
こういった見方は大まちがいもよいところです。日本は昔な
がらの孤立した殻に守ってもらうにはあまりにも大きくなり
すぎた生きもののようなものです。殻そのものを大きくして
いくことができかねる今日の時勢のもとにおいては、自分を
守るためには、それ以外の手だてを編み出していかねばなり
ません。日本がその繁栄をつづけ、平和のうちに生きのびて
いく唯一の方法が、国際化であることははっきりしています。
　したがって、今日の日本にとっての鍵[キーワード]となることばは、
国際化です。その真の意味を知り、そのもつ含みとともに問
題点をも知る必要があります。さもないと、日本が現在の繁
栄と経済的巨人としての世界的な主導権を保ちつづけること
などできません。いや、存立することさえできないのです。
私が、国際化が日本にとって何を意味し、それについて日本
人が考える際に考慮に入れるべきいくつかの問題点について
この小論をしたためたのも、実はこういう理由があればこそ
なのです。

　　　　　1988年　　3月13日

　　　　　　　　エドウィン・O・ライシャワー

CHAPTER 1

On Being a World Citizen
世界市民であること

CHAPTER 1

On Being a World Citizen

We all hear a great deal these days about the internation-alization of Japan and the need for individual Japanese to become more global in their attitudes—in other words, to become what Japanese call *kokusaijin*, or what in English we might call citizens of the world. This all sounds very fine, but actually just what does it mean? It seems very re-mote and theoretical, not something that actually affects the way we live. What does it have to do with our everyday lives, especially the lives of younger people? And just why is it necessary to become more international? How would each of us go about trying to achieve this goal? Can't inter-nationalization be left to statesmen and business leaders to worry about, leaving younger people free to concentrate on whatever may interest them, without concern for such big sounding but vague matters?

Many people feel that all this fuss about internation-alization is what Shakespeare called "Much Ado About

第1章

世界市民であること

　日本の国際化、そして一人一人の日本人の考え方がもっと地球大（グローバル）になることの必要性について、このところ何かと耳にするようになりました。つまりは日本人がいう「国際人」がこれで、英語だと「世界市民（シティズンズ・オブ・ザ・ワールド）」とでもいったらよいのでしょうか。ひびきはどれもたいへんに結構なのですが、それじゃいったいどういう意味なのでしょうか。ひどくかけはなれ、理屈っぽいように見え、われわれの生き方にかかわってくるようなものとは思えません。われわれの日々の暮し、とくに若い人々にとってどのようなかかわりがあるのでしょうか。そして、なぜもっと国際的にならなければいけないのでしょうか。この目標を達成するために、お互い一人一人がどのようにしたらよいのでしょうか。国際化なんて、政治や経済の指導者が気にすればよいことで、若い人々は何ごとであれ、自分たちの興味があることに熱中して、そんなご大層で何のことかピンとこないようなことには関心を示さない、というわけにはいかないのでしょうか。

　国際化についてのああでもない、こうでもないという騒ぎなど、シェイクスピアのいう『空騒ぎ』にすぎないと感じて

Nothing." Or else they believe that, whatever it may be, it is just too vast and remote a problem for them to do anything about. But if this is the way young Japanese actually do think, then they are making a serious mistake. The internationalization of Japan concerns the present life and immediate future of each individual Japanese. If younger people wait until they themselves have reached positions of leadership, they may find they have waited too long to solve the difficulties Japan might by then face. Internationalization is a challenge that confronts Japan and each individual Japanese right now.

It is for this reason that I hope you will join me in exploring what it means to be a world citizen, what are the problems this poses for Japan, and what each of you can do to face the challenge successfully. The role of younger Japanese is especially important, because they have more capacity to learn than do their elders, and it is they who will be the leaders of the future who must deal with the results of success or failure today in responding to the present situation.

いる人も少なくありません。そう思わぬまでも、いずれにせ
よ、これはあまりにも漠然としており自分たちとはかけはな
れた問題で、手のつけようがない、と信じている人もいます。
でももし日本の若い人々が実際このように考えているとする
なら、とても大きなあやまちをおかしていることになります。
日本の国際化は、日本人一人一人の今日の生活や近い未来に
かかわっているからです。もしも若い人々が、指導的な立場
に立つ日まで待つとしたら、そのときに日本が直面している
であろう諸問題を解決するのに、あまりにも待ち時間が長く
てもう手おくれだ、と思うことになるかもしれません。国際
化とは、日本と日本の個々人一人一人がいま向かい合ってい
る挑戦なのです。

　皆さんが私と一緒に、世界市民とは何を意味し、それが日
本にどのような問題をもたらし、この難問に立ち向かうため
にそれぞれ何ができるかを究めていってほしい、と願うのは
このためです。皆さんのような日本の若者の役割はとくに重
要です。皆さんの方が年長者よりも新しいものを身につける
容量が大きく、皆さんこそが明日の指導者であり、現在の状
況への対応が成功しても失敗しても、その成否の結果と対処
していかねばならないからです。

Westernization and Internationalization

In trying to define "internationalization," we must first dispose of one serious misconception. Many Japanese think it means the Westernization of Japanese life styles and values. They quite rightly see no need for this and feel that Japan has already shown itself to be the most open country in the world to foreign influences. In earlier times, Japanese drank deeply of Chinese culture, and in recent years Western cultural influences have poured into the land. For example, Japanese are now as familiar with Western music as with their own, and they probably have as great a mastery of it as do most of the peoples of the Occident. Foreign cultural influences, such as Chinese painting and Western literature, have greatly enriched Japan and have certainly made it culturally as international as any nation in the world.

Japan has also been fully open to foreign technology and as a result has now become a world leader in science and technology. The same is true of its political and social institutions as well as its urban, industrialized life styles.

西欧化と国際化

「国際化」ということばを定義するにあたり、一つの誤解を
まず片づけておかねばなりません。日本人の多くは、国際化
とは日本式の生活様式や価値感を西欧化することだと考えて
います。でも、彼らがそんな必要はないと思うのも当然でし
て、現に日本は外国からの影響に対し、世界でももっとも開
かれた国であると感じています。かつての日々に日本人は中
国文明をどっさり飲み干しました。そして近年に至り、欧米
の文化的な影響が日本に流れ入ってきました。一例ですが、
日本人は自分たちの音楽と同じくらいに、欧米の音楽に親し
んでおり、欧米の大部分の人々と同じほど、それをわがもの
にしています。中国の絵画や欧米の文学など外来の文化的影
響は、日本をうんと豊かにし、日本を他の国々にひけをとら
ぬほどの国際的な存在にしました。

　日本はまた、外来の技術に対しても完全に門戸を開いてき
ました。そのためいまや日本は科学・技術において世界の指
導的な立場に立つようになったのです。同じことは、都市化
し工業化した生活様式とともに、政治や社会面の機構につい

Although there is much that is distinctively Japanese in the way people live, the general patterns of modern city life in Japan are basically much like those of life in any of the advanced democracies in the world.

It should be obvious to anyone that Japan is unquestionably a very international country. No one could argue that it must make its patterns of trade more international or that it needs to make its culture or its lifestyle less Japanese and more Western. If Japan were to lose its Japanese identity, this would be a great loss not only for it but for the whole world. Japan's cultural distinctiveness enriches the world, and no one should wish to see it disappear like some endangered species of animal. That certainly cannot be the meaning of the internationalization that people are talking about. They clearly have something quite different in mind.

When I speak of internationalization, I do not mean the changing of external life styles but the development of internal new attitudes. Our motivations must be in step with the conditions of the time. For the two to be out of kilter with each other is a recipe for disaster, as Germany and Japan discovered in the Second World War.

てもいえます。人々の生き方には、明らかに日本的なものも
たくさん残ってはいますが、近代都市の生活の一般的な様式
は、世界の近代民主主義国のそれと、基本的にはよく似てい
ます。

　日本が疑いもなくうんと国際的な国であるという事実は、
だれの目にも明らかなはずです。通商の形態をもっと国際的
にすべきであるとか、文化や生活様式をもっと欧米流にして
日本色を薄めるべきだなどと主張することはできません。万
が一にも日本がその特異性（アイデンティティ）を失うようなことがあれば、そ
れは日本自身にとってだけでなく、世界全体にとっての大き
な損失となるでしょう。文化面での日本の際立った特色は、
世界を豊かなものにしており、絶滅に瀕した動物のように消
えてなくなることなど、だれも望んではいないはずです。皆
が口にしている国際化ということばの意味が、そのようなも
のであることはありえません。明らかにそれとは違ったなに
かを頭においているのです。

　私が国際化というときそれは、外見上の生活様式を変える
ことではなく、内面における新しい考え方を作り上げていく
ことを意味しているのです。私たちの動機とその時代の状況
とは歩調があっていなければなりません。この２つが噛み合
わない、ということは惨禍のためのかっこうの筋書となりま
す。第二次世界大戦当時の日本やドイツが気づいたとおりに
です。

World conditions are constantly changing, and attitudes must change with them. If they do not, catastrophe is bound to follow. The attitude that now is most in need of change is the way we view the relationship of ourselves and our countries to other lands. Not long ago it was possible to see ourselves simply as citizens of one country, and we regarded all other nations as potential enemies or at least hostile rivals. Such attitudes are dangerously out of date in a world in which the weapons of military destruction have become so terrible that their full use would destroy civilization and international economic relations have become so complex and interdependent that no country can stand alone. We must see ourselves as citizens of a world community of nations which cooperate with one another for their common good. For Japan, which has become one of the economic giants of the world, these new attitudes have to include a willingness to play a much larger role in world affairs than it has in the past. This is the true meaning of internationalization and world citizenship.

　世界の状況はたえず変化しており、考え方もそれにともなって変わっていかなければなりません。いまいちばん変わる必要があるのは、自分や自分たちの国と他の国々との関係をどう見るかという点です。比較的最近までは、自分たちをある国の市民とだけ考えることも可能でした。他国民なんて、潜在的な敵か、そこまでいかないまでも、敵意をもった競争相手（ライバル）とみなしたものです。しかし今日のように、軍事的な破壊手段が恐ろしいものとなり、これをフルに使えば文明そのものを破滅させてしまうことができ、また国際的な経済関係が複雑かつ相互依存度の高いものとなり、どの国もひとりぼっちでは成り立っていかなくなった時代にあっては、このような考え方は、危険なまでに時代遅れとなっています。われわれは、自分たちを共通の善のために互いに協力しあう諸国民による世界的な連合の市民とみなさなければなりません。いまや世界でも経済的な巨人の一員となった日本にとっては、このような新しい考え方は、従来よりも世界のことがらについてはるかに大きな役割を果たすという意欲を含むものでなければなりません。これが国際化と世界市民ということの、真の意味なのです。

The Development of Human Society

I can perhaps make the point clearer by giving a thumb-nail sketch of man's evolutionary progress. In primitive times, people survived by living in groups. At first, these were largely one or more families who hunted, gathered food, and cared for each other together. Even today the family remains as a primary unit for individual survival and social organization.

Gradually, as people acquired greater skills and abilities at organization, family groupings grew into larger and more complex organizations. In some cases, tribal bands developed into very large and even powerful organizations, like the German tribes of Europe which overran the Roman Empire and the semi-nomadic Mongol tribes which conquered most of Asia and part of Europe. The early Japanese uji are probably to be classified as a variant of this tribal pattern, and in many of the more backward parts of the world tribal organizations still linger on.

Agriculture brought a new unit of organization—the farming village—in which related and unrelated families

人間社会の発展

　この点をいま少しはっきりさせるために、ヒトがどのよう
な進化の過程をたどってきたかについて、簡単な描写^{スケッチ}をここ
ろみておきます。未開時代にあっては、人々は集団で生きる
ことで生命をつないでいました。最初は、一家族もしくは数
家族が、共同で獲物を狩ったり、食物を集めたり、お互いに
めんどうをみあうという形が主でした。今日にあっても、個
人の生存と社会的な組織のための主たる単位といえば、やは
り家族です。

　やがて人々が多くの技能や組織上の能力を加えるにともな
って、家族から成る集団は、より大きく、より複雑な組織体
へと発展していきました。時と場合によっては、部族的な集
団が巨大で、しかも強力でさえある組織体へと形を変えてい
ったのです。ヨーロッパではローマ帝国を席巻したゲルマン
の諸部族、またアジアのほとんどとヨーロッパの一部分を征
服した、半遊牧民族のモンゴールの諸部族などが、その例で
す。初期の日本の「氏^{うじ}」も、おそらくはこの部族的な形態の
一変形に分類されるべきでしょうし、また世界の遅れた地域
の多くにあっては、いまなお部族的な組織体が生き残ってい
ます。

　農業は新しい組織単位をもたらしました。農耕村落がこれ

cooperated on many matters, such as the fair distribution of water and their joint defense against raiders. Some villages, especially those at key spots on trade routes, developed into little cities protected by walls and ruling over surrounding farming communities. Such walled city-states were scattered widely in ancient times in such places as North China, Northwest India, and the Mediterranean region in the West.

Man's progress in making weapons and tools, first of bronze and then of iron, accompanied the development of agriculture and the domestication of horses, sheep, and oxen. Together these innovations permitted the growth of much larger, more powerful, and more complex social and political institutions. Great empires appeared in very ancient times in Egypt, Mesopotamia, and probably India, and later spread through the Middle East, the eastern Mediterranean, and China. The age of ancient empires culminated in the long-lasting Roman Empire in the West and the even more durable Chinese Empire in the East.

Human inventions continued, creating new possibilities and also new problems. Sometimes they undermined old institutions, such as the Roman Empire, but new institu-

で、そこでは血縁のある家族もない家族も、皆がさまざまな
ことがらで力を合わせました。水を公平に分配するとか、共
同で侵入者に備えるということなどがそれです。このような
村落の一部で、とくに通商上の主要な道筋にあったものは、
小都市へと発展していきました。壁をめぐらし、近隣の農耕
社会を支配することで自らを守っていたのです。これらの防
壁をめぐらした都市国家は、古代においては中国の北部、イ
ンドの北西部、そして欧米では地中海地域など、世界の各地
に散在していました。

　ヒトが最初は青銅、ついでは鉄による武器や道具類を作れ
るようになったことは、農業の発達やウマ、ヒツジ、ウシな
どの家畜化をともないました。このような技術革新が相まっ
て、より大きく、より強力で、より複雑な、社会的政治的な
機構の発展を可能にしました。ごくごく古代において、巨大
帝国がエジプトやメソポタミア、そしておそらくはインドに
生まれ、やがて中近東や地中海の東部、そして中国へと拡が
っていきました。これら古代帝国の時代に全盛をきわめたの
は、西洋においては長期にわたって存続したローマ帝国、そ
して東洋においては持続度がより高い中国（の諸王朝が作り
出した）帝国でした。

　人間による発明がひきつづき、新しい可能性とともに新し
い問題を生み出していきました。ときにはこれらの問題が、
ローマ帝国のような古い機構を掘り崩していくこともありま
したが、いつも新しい機構が生まれては、とって代わってい

27

tions always rose to take their place. Always the appearance of new technologies required the development of new ideas and new social and political patterns. Human civilization constantly kept evolving. The feudal pattern of life in Europe and Japan was one of these innovations brought by technological changes and altered conditions of life. In modern times, the nation state, usually centering around a shared language, became the primary focus of political organization, sweeping away older organizations by tribal units, personal loyalties to ruling families, or shared religious beliefs.

Nationalism now dominates almost all parts of the world. This can well be called the age of nationalism. But it is not hard to see that we are approaching the end of that age. No one can deny that mankind has made stunning progress under the nation state during the past few centuries, but it is becoming clear that the continuation much longer of an unbridled system of mutually antagonistic national units would bring us to catastrophe. The First and Second World Wars were fought well before most of you were born, but actually not very long ago in historic terms. Both occurred during my lifetime, and most people would agree that a Third World War would bring an end

ったのです。新しい技術が現われると、新しい思想や社会的
政治的な形態の発展が必要とされるのが常でした。人間の文
明はたえず変化していきました。ヨーロッパや日本での封建
的な生活形態は、技術上の変化や生活条件の変更が生み出し
た革新の一つだったのです。近代になりますと、だいたいは
一つの言語の共有を軸とする民族国家が、政治的な組織の中
心となり、部族的な単位や支配的な家族への忠誠、もしくは
宗教的な信条の共有による古い形の組織体を追い払ってしま
ったのです。

　いまではナショナリズムが世界のほとんどすべての地域を
支配しています。今日はナショナリズムの時代と呼ぶべきか
もしれません。しかしこういった時代の終末に近づきつつあ
ることに気づくのは、むずかしいことではありません。民族
国家のもと、ここ数世紀の間に人類が驚くほどの進歩をとげ
たことはだれも否定できません。でも、お互いに敵対しあう
民族的単位がなんの制約もなしにこれ以上長期にわたって続
くようなら、われわれに破滅がもたらされることが明らかに
なりつつあるのです。第一次、第二次の二度の世界大戦が戦
われたのは、皆さんのほとんどが生まれるずっと以前のこと
ですが、でも歴史的な物差しでいうなら、それほど昔のこと
ではありません。いずれも私の一生涯のうちのできごとです
し、もし第三次世界大戦が起きるようなら、お互いが知って

to civilization as we know it. In fact, it might mean the extinction of the whole human race. For the first time in history we are very close to the brink of our own self-destruction.

The reasons for our perilous position are quite clear. It is the result of rapid technological changes which, just as in the past, demand new solutions for new problems. These in turn require new attitudes and new institutions. There is no stopping the forward motion of science and technology, even if we wished to do so. Science and technology will continue to make rapid progress, but they will not solve all difficulties, as many people seem to think. They may help alleviate certain specific problems, such as the control of some diseases, the need for more food, or even the development of new and better sources of energy, such as photoelectric power from sunshine. But the really dangerous problems are only made more pressing.

Take nuclear power for example. More destructive and accurate nuclear weapons only make our dangers greater. Expanding nuclear defense or offense systems into space makes the situation more complex and therefore more hazardous. What is obviously needed

いるような意味での文明が終末を迎えるという点については、ほとんどの人が同意することでしょう。それだけではなく、全人類の滅亡すら意味しかねません。歴史始まって以来はじめて、われわれは自己破壊の深淵の目と鼻のところにいるのです。

なぜこのような危なっかしい立場にあるのか、その理由はきわめてはっきりしています。それは急激な技術面での変化の結果であり、過去におけると同様、新しい問題に対する新しい解決策が必要とされるのです。そのためには、新しい考え方や新しい機構が求められます。たとえそう望んだとしても、科学や技術が前進していくのをとどめることはできません。科学技術はこれからも急速な前進を続けていくでしょう。しかし、多くの人々はそれがすべての困難を解決してくれると思っているようですが、そうはいきません。ある種の病気を押さえこむとか、もっと食料をという必要を充たすとか、太陽光線をつかった光電気エネルギーなどよりよい新エネルギー源を開発することを含め、いくつかの特定の問題の軽減には役立つかもしれません。でもほんとうに危険な問題はむしろもっと緊急なものになっています。

一例として原子力を考えてみましょう。破壊的で精度の高い核兵器が増えることは、われわれの危険を大きくするばかりです。核兵器による防衛用ないしは攻撃用のシステムを宇宙空間に拡げていくことは、状況をもっと複雑な、それだけにより危険なものにします。明らかに必要とされているのは、

are new worldwide concepts of international cooperation. Clearly, our only salvation is new attitudes and
institutions.

The same is true of the other major areas in which the
future of mankind is threatened. World problems are extremely diverse and complicated, but we might concentrate
our discussion on three of the most dangerous areas. The
first and most clear-cut is military defense and particularly
the problem of nuclear weapons, which I have just mentioned. The second is the increasingly complex and crucial
problem of international economic relations, especially
among the advanced industrialized nations. The third is
the swelling world population and the growing gulf between the poverty of the fast growing populations of the
poor and backward nations and the more static demo-
graphic conditions of the rich and advanced countries.

The economies of the more advanced industrial nations have become so interdependent that these countries
all depend on each other for their prosperity or in some
cases for their very existence. Japan is a good case in point.
It could not survive without tremendous imports from
abroad and vast overseas markets to pay for these imports.

新しい世界大での国際協力という考え方です。われわれにとっての唯一の救いが、新しい考え方や機構にあることははっきりしています。

　人類の将来が脅かされている他の主だった分野についても同じことがいえます。世界の問題はきわめて多様で入りくんだものですが、私はここでもっとも危険の多い諸分野を3つに絞って考えてみようと思います。最初に、もっとも明白なのは軍備、なかでも核兵器の問題で、これについてはさきほど述べたとおりです。第2は複雑の度を加える一方で決定的に重要な問題となっている国際的な経済関係、それもとくに先進工業国同士のそれです。第3は世界人口がふくれあがり、人口が急速に伸びつつある貧しい後進国の貧困と、人口が安定している先進諸国の豊かさとの格差が拡がりつつあるという点です。

　先進工業諸国の経済が相互依存度を深めたために、これらの国々は自国の繁栄はもとより、時によっては存立のためにも、お互いを必要としています。日本はそのかっこうの例です。外国からの莫大な輸入や、そのための外貨を入手するための巨大な海外市場がなければ、日本の存続はありえません。日本はエネルギー資源の大半を海外に仰いでおり、衣料用の

The great bulk of its energy resources comes from abroad, as well as most of its material for clothing, the materials for its machinery and manufactured goods, the wood for its domestic housing and paper, the fertilizers and feed grains for food production, and much of the food its people consume. Without an extensive worldwide trading system, the majority of the Japanese people probably could not be kept alive even at subsistence levels. Other geographically larger countries like the United States, Canada, and Australia, might be better able to survive than Japan but only at drastically reduced levels of well-being.

As the world economy has become more complex and interdependent, we have witnessed a sharp rise in economic frictions between the industrialized countries and a growing tendency of economic conditions in one to influence conditions in the others. It has become abundantly clear that we are all in the same economic boat together. If one part of it starts to sink, the whole boat will founder. We cannot allow frictions between us to divert our attention from the maintenance of our craft. Trade wars between us would be like punching holes in the bottom of our rival's portion of the boat. The water that would seep in would

原料にしても、機械や製品の原料にしても、国内住宅や製紙用の木材にしても、食料生産用の肥料や飼料穀物にしても、国民が消費する食料の多くにしても、同じことがいえます。世界大の通商システムが張りめぐらされていなければ、日本人の大多数は生存すれすれのレベルですら生きていくことはできないにちがいありません。アメリカ合衆国やカナダやオーストラリアのように面積の大きな国なら日本よりは生き抜いていきやすいかもしれませんが、それでもその生活状態のレベルが際立って低くなることは必至です。

　世界経済が複雑さと相互依存の度を加えるにともなって、工業国家間の経済面での葛藤が急増し、一国の経済状態が他の国々の状態に影響する度合が高まるのを目のあたりにしてきました。われわれは皆、いわば「経済」という同じ船に乗り組んでいることが明明白白となってきました。その船の一部が沈みはじめるようだと、船全体が破船してしまいます。お互い同士の葛藤に心を奪われて、船の保守管理をおろそかにしてはなりません。先進国同士の貿易戦争というのは、いってみればお互いの船の相手側の部分に穴をあけるようなものです。そこから水が入ってきて船全体が浸水し、やがてはみんな一緒に沈んでしまうことになってしまいます。密接な協力と、お互いに運命を一つにしているという認識を分かち

soon fill the whole boat and we would all go down together. Here obviously is an area that demands close cooperation and a shared view of our common fate. We can no longer act purely in our own narrow self-interest, but must approach our economic problems in a more international way as responsible world citizens.

Today we are already confronted by serious problems of economic coordination and cooperation among the advanced industrialized countries, but, if we extend our vision a little further into the future, we can see a still graver and more difficult problem lying ahead. This is the gap between the rich industrialized nations of the so-called first world and the impoverished, under-industrialized countries of the so-called third world, which consists of a large group of nations, running from primitive little states in Africa through the great historic giants of India and China to the relatively prosperous though unstable countries of Latin America. They are culturally so diverse as to defy easy characterization, but some generalizations can be made about them. Together they constitute about three quarters of the world's population and are growing much faster than the rest of

あうことが、ここで求められるのは明らかです。われわれは
もはや自分たちだけの狭い利益だけで行動することはできま
せん。責任ある世界市民として、お互いの経済問題にもっと
国際的なやり方であたっていかなければならないのです。

　今日ですらわれわれは先進国同士の経済調整とか協力とい
う深刻な問題にぶつかっているのですが、目をもう少し未来
に向けるなら、より重大で困難な問題が前途に横たわってい
るのがわかります。それはいわゆる第一世界の豊かな工業国
家と、いわゆる第三世界の貧しい工業化の遅れた国々との格
差です。しかも後者はアフリカの未開な小国から、インドや
中国という歴史的な巨人を経て、比較的豊かではありながら
安定を欠くラテンアメリカの諸国に及ぶ、たくさんの国々を
含んでいます。文化的にきわめて多岐にわたるので、単純な
性格づけを許しませんが、それでも多少の一般化は可能です。
これらの国々を合わせますと、世界総人口の４分の３を占め、
しかもその人口増加率は他の地域よりうんと高いのです。い
ずれも程度の差こそあれ深刻な貧困に悩まされており、高度
工業国家におくれをとる一方である、というのがそのほとん
どです。したがって、非常に不安定で、先進国は自分たちを
不当に搾取しているとして恨みを抱いています。

the world. They all suffer more or less seriously from poverty and are, for the most part, falling ever further behind the advanced industrialized nations. They are accordingly unstable themselves and resentful of the richer countries, which they feel exploit them unfairly.

This situation will become increasingly dangerous as the whole world becomes ever more interdependent, the relative size of the third world grows, and weapons of destruction and the possibilities for disruption in our increasingly complex world system become steadily greater. Here is another area for grave concern. Ways must be found to head off a seemingly inevitable clash between the poor and rich countries. We must learn how to help the third world countries achieve prosperity and more satisfactory participation in the world economic system. The problems are so diverse and complex that it would be impossible in the short time we have to attempt to outline specific solutions, but the first step that should be taken is obvious. We must view these problems, not in the light of narrow national interests, but from an international point of view. In their words, we must approach them in the spirit of world citizens. Here is another aspect of the true meaning of internationalization.

　世界全体が相互依存の度合を深め、第三世界が相対的に大きくなり、破壊用の兵器や、複雑になる一方の世界システムにおける崩壊の可能性が高まる一方とあっては、この第三世界をめぐる状況はますますもって危険なものになっていくでしょう。これまた深刻な懸念を抱かされる分野です。貧しい国々と豊かな国々との間の不可避と思われる衝突を未然に防ぐ手だてが見つけられなければなりません。われわれは第三世界が繁栄を手に入れ、世界の経済システムにもっと満足のいく形で参加できるよう、手を貸すにはどうしたらよいかを探っていかねばなりません。問題があまりにも多岐にわたり複雑をきわめるので、具体的な解決策を呈示しようとしても、限られた時間内では不可能ですが、まず何がなされなければならないか、というその第一段階ははっきりしています。われわれはこれらの諸問題を、自分たちの国益という狭い視点から見るのではなく、国際的な見地から見ていかねばなりません。ことばを変えていうなら、世界市民という精神にのっとって問題への接近をはかるべきなのです。これが国際化ということばの真の意味の、いま一つの側面なのです。

Individual Attitudes

Up until now I have been speaking in general terms about great trends in history and problems that concern the world as a whole. All this may not seem to have much to do with our own daily lives. It is somewhat like reading a novel about other people. In a way it resembles the weather, which we can observe with pleasure or dismay, but over which we have no control. On the contrary, however, world history is not a spectator sport. The world's peoples are all players, and the outcomes depend on what we all do individually as well as collectively.

The problems we face are admittedly global and can only be solved through international relations, national policies, the actions of great economic corporations, and worldwide cultural contacts. Each of you naturally feels powerless in the face of such great forces, like King Canute who sought to stem the rising tide. But you all will suffer individually from mistakes in national and international policies or else will gain individually from their wisdom.

個々人の考え方

　これまでのところ私は、歴史の大きな流れと全世界にかかわりのある問題点について、ごく一般的な話をしてきました。こういったことがらは、われわれの日常生活とはたいした関係があるようには見えないかもしれません。他の人々についての小説を読むのと一脈通じていなくもありません。お天気と似ている面もあります。よかったと思ったり、顔をしかめたりのどちらかであっても、手の打ちようがない、という点でです。でも世界歴史というのは単なる観るスポーツではありません。すべての人々が参加するスポーツで、どういう結果が出るかは、われわれが個人として、また集団として何をするかによって決まるのです。

　われわれが向かい合っている問題が地球大のものであることはいうまでもなく、それだけに国際的な関係、国家ごとの政策、大企業などの経済組織の行動、それに世界にまたがった文化交流などを通じてしか解決できないのです。このような巨大な勢力を前にして、皆さん一人一人が無力感にとらわれるのも、しごくもっともです。潮が満ちてくるのを押しとどめようとしたというかのカヌート王さながらにです。でも、国家次元や国際次元の政策のあやまりは皆さん個人個人をひ

Basically, it is the mass of individual people who determine what a country or any group is able or willing to do. Individuals are the foundation for any system, and their attitudes determine the policies of the nation or group to which they belong. In the long run, nothing is more important than the attitudes of individual people.

From what I have said, it is clear that the starting point for internationalization and the development of a sense of being a world citizen is the attitude each one of you takes. Though the problems may seem so huge as to be far beyond your personal reach, each of you can make a contribution by developing the knowledge and viewpoints required by the situation. The greater your knowledge and understanding, the more you can contribute, not only by the firmness of your own beliefs, but by your ability to set an example for others.

How can you go about developing the needed knowledge and appropriate attitudes? A person's attention quite naturally is at first focused on himself and his immediate surroundings. This is true of all small children, who are concerned only with themselves and their own families. Only as they grow older is their interest gradually drawn to more distant fields—their immediate community, their

どい目にあわせるでしょうし、その逆に政策面での英知のお
かげで一人一人がうるおう、ということもあるでしょう。一
つの国であれ集団であれ、どのようなことができ、またやる
気があるかを決めるものは、基本的には一人一人の個人が形
づくる一群の人々なのです。どのようなシステムにしろ、そ
の基礎にあるのは個人なので、個人の考え方がその人たちの
国なり集団なりの政策を決めていくのです。長い目で見るな
ら、個々人の考え方ぐらい大事なものはないといえます。

　ここまでお話ししてきたことで、国際化ならびに世界市民
という感覚の涵養にとっての第一歩が、皆さん一人一人がど
のような姿勢をとるかである、ということがはっきりしまし
た。問題があまりにも巨大にすぎ、とても個人の力の及ぶと
ころではないように見えますが、この状況が必要とするよう
な知識や視点を養っていくことで、皆さん一人一人が貢献す
ることもできるのです。皆さんの知識や理解が大きければ大
きいほど、自分自身の確固たる信念だけでなく、他者の手本
になれるという能力によっても、より大きな貢献をすること
が可能です。

　ではどのようにしたら必要とされる知識やしかるべき考え
方を身につけていくことができるのでしょうか。人間の関心
がまず自分自身とその身の回りに向けられるのは、しごく当
り前です。小さい子どもというのは全部がそうして、自分
と自分の家族にしか関心を示しません。もっと離れた分野、
たとえば身近な地域社会、学校、会社、町や地域、そして自

school, their company, their town or region, and finally to their country. Up to this level, the educational system helps lead them into these broader fields of concern. But there it stops. No organized system induces people to take the next step to a concern about the world and humanity as a whole, even though it is now quite evident that the unit of survival is becoming, not the individual country, but the world as a whole. You have to take this next step largely on your own. This requires a self-conscious effort to widen your focus of vision and see the world as a whole or at least from more than one point of view.

How can you do this? It seems particularly difficult for Japanese, because they have a strong sense of being an isolated island people, extremely homogeneous and with unique qualities that set them apart from all other national groups. It should be admitted that there is some basis for this attitude. Until men fully mastered oceanic travel in the sixteenth century, the Japanese were geographically one of the most isolated of the large groups of people in the world. This natural isolation permitted them to continue until relatively recent times an artificial isolation under the Tokugawa shogunate.

分の国といった対象がはじめて関心をひくようになるのは、成長するにしたがってです。この段階までは、教育制度がこれらより広範な関心分野へとわれわれが向かうのを助けてくれます。でもその追跡はここでストップしてしまいます。世界や人類全体についての関心という、次の段階に人々を誘ってくれる組織化されたシステムなどないのです。存続のための単位が個々の国ではなく、世界全体になりつつあることが、いまや明白なのにもかかわらずです。ですからこの次の段階は、おおむね独力でとびこえなければならないのです。そのためには視野を広げ、世界を全体として捉える、少なくとも一つの視点だけにこだわらないように、意識的に努力することが必要とされます。

　では、どうしたらこうできるのでしょうか。日本人にとってはとくに困難なように思われます。日本人は、自分たちを孤絶した島国の民で、きわめて均質的なうえに、他の民族集団とはへだたったユニークな資質の持ち主だとみなしているからです。このような考え方には何がしかの根拠があることは否定できません。16世紀に至り、人間が大海航行のための技術を完全にマスターするまで、日本人というのは、世界の中でももっとも孤立した大集団の一つだったのです。この自然の孤立状態があったために、比較的最近に至るまで日本は徳川幕府下においての人為的な鎖国をつづけることができたのでした。

Another factor is the Japanese language, which differs radically from most of the other major languages of the world. Given the geographic and linguistic isolation of Japan, it is not at all surprising that the Japanese should have developed one of the most distinctive cultures in the world and a particularly strong sense of self-identity. But all nations are in some ways distinctive and have a sense of being unique. Japanese may have this feeling more strongly than most, but this is only a matter of a difference in degree, not in kind. We should not forget that the greater part of most of Japanese traditional culture has close parallels in the neighboring lands of China and Korea and its modern culture is much like that of the other advanced industrialized democracies. Japanese may find it more difficult than most people to view the world impartially from outside their own national setting, but their problem in being world citizens is essentially no different from that faced by all the peoples of the world.

　いま一つの要因は日本語です。世界の主要言語のどれとも、きわめて異なっているのが日本語です。地理的にも言語の面でも孤立していることを思えば、日本人が世界でももっとも特徴のはっきりした文化を生み出し、強い自意識を持っているのも驚くにはあたりません。でも世界の国民はすべて自分たちが、何らかの面で特異性をもち、ユニークであると思っています。日本人のほうがその度合は強いかもしれません。でもそうはいってもことは程度の差であって、質の違いではないのです。日本の伝統文化のほとんどについて、その大部分が中国や朝鮮などの近隣の地域にごく類似した存在があること、そして、その現代文化が他の高度工業民主主義国のそれとよく似ていることを忘れるべきではありません。自分たちの国家的次元から一歩離れて世界を客体視することは、日本人にとっては他の人々よりも困難を感じることかもしれません。でも、世界市民になるうえに日本人がかかえる問題は、他の諸国民がかかえているものと、本質においては何ら異なっていないのです。

Specific Steps

To return to the question of how each of us can internationalize ourselves and become world citizens, the first step obviously is to acquire broader knowledge. We all need to know more about the rest of the world and how other people think. Facts and statistics are of course important, but they are relatively easy to acquire. What is more important is to learn how other people regard their problems and their relations with the rest of the world.

What is the best way to do this? There is a great deal that can be learned from reading newspapers, magazines, works of literature, scholarly books, or more popular travel accounts. Good documentary programs on television can also be helpful. But it should be remembered that what Japanese write for other Japanese is likely to be colored by Japanese psychology and therefore may reenforce your prejudices more than they broaden your focus of vision. For this reason books and programs by foreigners, especially those by the natives of the country under consideration, are more

具体的な段階と手だて

　お互い一人一人がどうしたら国際化し世界市民に自分を仕立てていけるかという問題に戻るとして、第1の段階がより広範な知識を手に入れることにあるのは明白です。自分以外の世界や、他の人々がどう考えているかについてもっと知る必要があります。事実や統計数字もむろん大切です。しかし、それらは比較的手に入りやすいものです。もっと大切なのは、他の人々が自分たちの問題や世界との関係をどのように見ているか、を知ることなのです。

　そのためのいちばんよい方法は何でしょうか。新聞や雑誌、文学作品や学問的著作、さらにはもっと一般的な旅行記を通じて知ることのできることはたくさんあります。すぐれたテレビのドキュメンタリー番組も有益です。でも忘れてならないことは、日本人が日本人向けに書くものは、日本的な心理に色どられており、それだけに皆さんの視野を広げるよりは、むしろ逆に偏見を強めることになりかねないということです。ですから外国人の著作や番組、とくに対象となる国の人の手になるものは、新しい洞察をものにするうえにもっと役立ちます。びっくりするほど違った見方のため、ショックを受けることがあるかもしれません。ひどくまちがっていることも

likely to help one gain new insights. They may shock you by their startlingly different points of view. Perhaps they may be seriously mistaken, but at least they show what other people are thinking. The very shock of their very different attitudes may be helpful in freeing you from some hitherto unchallenged assumptions or may open unexpected new vistas.

It must be admitted, of course, that appropriate books and programs do not exist for all regions. In fact, they are probably missing for most, and whole problem areas may simply be overlooked by the writers of books. I know there are many questions about which I wish to know more, but find no books to guide me. There are stacks of books about the attitudes of the great military and economic powers toward even small and remote parts of the world, but what is in the mind of the average North Korean worker, Chinese peasant, Filipino villager, Malay, Indian, or Chinese citizen of Malaysia, Burmese tribesman, Indian untouchable, Soviet Moslem, Iranian townsman, Arab-speaking citizen of any one of a dozen different Arab lands, a member of one of the hundreds of tribes divided between recently established countries in Africa, or Latin American peasants in one of

ありえましょう。しかし、それらは少なくとも外の人々が何を思っているかを知らせてくれます。まったくちがった考え方に触れたショックはかえって、いままでは疑ってもみなかった思い込みから皆さんを解き放ち、想像もしなかったような新しい視点を開いてくれることになるかもしれません。

　世界のあらゆる地域について、しかるべき書物や番組が存在するわけでないことは、残念ながら事実です。それどころか、ほとんどの地域についてそんなものはない、というのがおそらくは事実で、物書きがいくつもの問題地域をまったく無視しているということもあるでしょう。現に私ももっとくわしく知りたいと思う問題が数多くあっても、私を導いてくれる本が一つもないようなことがよくあります。軍事的経済的な大国が、世界中のいとささやかでもっとも遠隔の地域についてどのように考えているかを教えてくれる本は山のようにあります。でも平均的な北朝鮮の労働者や中国人の農民、フィリピンの村人やマレー系、インド系、中国系のマレーシア市民、ビルマの少数部族やインドの不可触賤民、ソビエトのイスラム教徒やイランの町民、十いくつものアラブ諸国においてアラブ語をしゃべる市民やアフリカの新興独立国家の間で引き裂かれた何百何千という部族の一人一人そして西半球の数多くのスペイン諸国家のラテン系の小農民などは、い

51

the many Spanish speaking lands in the Western Hemisphere? What do these people worry about and hope for? Even people who are close to us in lifestyles and ways of thinking are hard to understand. The same set of facts may appear very differently to Japanese and Americans, Englishmen and Frenchmen, Finns and Germans, Italians and Swiss. We face a never-ending task of trying to expand our knowledge and understanding of the rest of the world.

In addition to study, another important way to increase our knowledge and understanding of other peoples is to develop every contact we can with the outside world. Travel is one obvious way to do this, but special efforts are needed to keep it from being superficial. A quick tourist trip can teach us about the airports and international hotels of the world, the outside appearance of a few large cities, and possibly about some of the art treasures and beauty spots of the world, but if that is all we see, we have not done much better than to look at a picture book or visit a museum. We need to get off the beaten tourist track and meet people and learn something of their lives and thoughts. This requires special effort and an ability to overcome the language barrier.

ったい何を思っているのでしょうか。彼らは何を気に病み、望んでいるのでしょうか。われわれと生活様式や考え方がよく似ている人々ですら、理解がむずかしいのです。同じような一連の事実についてですら、日本人と合衆国人、イギリス人とフランス人、フィンランド人とドイツ人、イタリア人とスイス人では、うんと違って見えるのです。自分以外の世界に関する知識や理解を深めるという、終わることのない仕事と、われわれは向かい合っているのです。

　勉強のほかに他の国民についての知識や理解を増していくうえのいま一つの大切な方法は、外部世界との交流を一つ一つ深めていくことです。旅行というのがそのための手っとりばやい方法の一つであることははっきりしていますが、単に表面的なことに終わらせないためには、格別な努力が必要とされます。観光客としてのあわただしい旅行は、なるほど空港や国際ホテル、いくつかの大都市の外観、それにあるいは世界的な美術品や名所のいくらかについて物を教えてくれはします。でもその程度にとどまるとするなら、写真集を手にしたり美術館を訪れるのとたいした差はありません。月並みな観光ルートから離れ、土地の人々に会うことで、彼らがどのような生活を営み、何を考えているのかについて、多少は知ることが肝心です。そのためには格段の努力が要りますし、ことばの壁を乗り越える能力も必要です。

We can also take advantage of foreigners who live in our country. Most Japanese find it embarrassing or irksome to establish close contacts with foreigners, but this is a means of education that should not be overlooked. Foreigners should be sought out, not shunned. Many young Japanese are willing to try to cultivate English-speaking acquaintances for the help they can be in language learning, but they avoid Koreans and Chinese who live in Japan in much greater numbers. This is a serious mistake. To learn what Koreans or Chinese think is an important first step in getting away from a purely Japan-bound point of view and developing a more international outlook on world problems.

The second step that should be taken is more difficult than the mere accumulation of knowledge about conditions and attitudes in other parts of the world. This is to make a conscious effort to see problems from the various points of view of other peoples in the world. You should try to imagine yourself to be a member of some other national group and then regard the relations of that country with Japan or its attitudes toward some difficulty it faces. The world and its problems obviously look

　在留外国人の存在を利用することもできます。外国人と近しい関係を結ぶことが、ほとんどの日本人にとって、恥ずかしかったり気づまりだったりするのはたしかですが、これは見すごすことのできない教育手段の一つです。外国人はこちらのほうからかかわっていくべきで、背中を向けるべきではありません。日本の若者の多くは、ことばの学習の一助として、英語を話す外国人と知り合うことには前向きですが、もっと多数の在日朝鮮・韓国人や中国人は避けて通ります。これは大きなまちがいです。朝鮮・韓国人や中国人が何を考えているかを学ぶことは、日本だけにこりかたまった狭い視野から離れて、世界の諸問題に関するもっと国際的な視点を作り上げていくうえの、重要な一段階です。

　踏むべき第２の段階は、外国の状態や考え方について単に知識を蓄積するよりも、実はもっとむずかしいことです。世界の諸国民の異なる視点から問題を見ることができるよう、意識的な努力を払う、というのがこれです。つまり、日本人以外の民族集団の一員の立場に自分自身をまず置き、次にその国と日本との関係ないしはその国が直面している困難について思いをはせるのです。世界と世界がかかえている諸問題についての日本人や合衆国人の見方は、イラン人やエジプト人、南アフリカの白人や黒人、ブラジル人やジャマイカ島民、

very different from the points of view of an Iranian, an Egyptian, a white or black South African, a Brazilian, a Jamaican, a Thailander, an Indian Sikh, a Siberian factory worker, a Pole, an Italian, a Swede, or a Palestinian than it does from that of a Japanese or an American. None of their points of view may be any more correct than your own and may possibly be much more distorted. But, if you can understand them even a little, you will be better able to make your own attitudes a bit more realistic and in line with the realities of the world. You would have moved somewhat closer to being a world citizen and making your country more international in a way that is important for everybody.

One final word: What I have been saying does not apply simply to Japan. It is true for all countries. But it applies particularly to the dominating economic and military powers of the world, particularly those that qualify as the leading members of the advanced first world. They must take the lead in such matters because they exercise much greater international influence than do less developed, economically more self-contained, or smaller countries. Japan and the United States are prime examples of advanced

タイ人や、シーク教徒のインド人、シベリアの工場労働者や
ポーランド人、イタリア人やスウェーデン人、そしてパレス
チナ人のそれとはうんと違っているであろうことははっきり
しています。彼らの見方が皆さんの見方より正しいという決
まりはありませんし、もっとゆがんだものである可能性もあ
ります。でもそれらを少しでも理解すれば、自分自身の考え
方をもう少し世界の実情に則した、より現実的なものに作り
上げていきやすくなるでしょう。つまりは世界市民に多少な
りと近づき、すべての人々にとって重要な形において日本を
より国際的な国に仕立てることができる、というわけなので
す。

　最後にひとこと。いままで私が述べてきたことは、日本に
だけあてはまるわけではありません。すべての国にあてはま
るのです。ただ経済や軍事の面で世界で支配的な地位にある
国々、なかでも高度に進歩した第一世界にあって主導的な立
場にある国々にはとくにあてはまります。これらのことがら
について主導権をとらねばならないのはこれらの国々なので
す。低開発国や、経済的に自己完結的な国々、ないしは小国
よりも、国際的な影響力がぐんと大きいからです。日本とア
メリカ合衆国とは、国際化ならびに世界市民という感覚の涵
養という面において、主導的な役割を演ずべき先進世界国家

world powers that should take the lead in internationalization and the development of a sense of world citizenship. But as I have said before, this can only be done through the attitudes of individual Japanese and Americans. It is the duty of each of you individually to increase your knowledge and understanding of the people of the world and to build on this a solid sense of world citizenship.

の、主だった存在です。ただすでに述べたように、個々の日本人や合衆国人の考え方を通してのみ、それは可能なのです。世界の人々についての知識や理解を増進し、そのうえに世界市民という確固とした認識を打ち立てるのは、皆さんたち一人一人の義務なのです。

What Can Japan Contribute to the World

日本は世界に何を寄与できるか

CHAPTER 2

What Can Japan Contribute
to the World?

In our first chapter about internationalization and world citizenship, we saw that the time was clearly past when countries and individuals could think only about their own narrow national interests. Now they must view things in terms of international cooperation and the security and wellbeing of mankind as a whole. It is also obvious that internationalization doesn't mean for Japan the abandonment of its own values and ways of life or any loss of identity. Quite on the contrary, it suggests the strengthening of certain Japanese characteristics so that they can serve as contributions by Japan to a more peaceful, stable, and prosperous world.

Another change in thinking the Japanese need to make is to become aware of Japan's position in the global community as one of the world's economic superpowers. Japanese must be more willing to assume an appropriate portion of the world's problems. In large part this

第2章

日本は世界に何を寄与できるか

　国際化と世界市民についての第1章で、国家や個人がそれぞれの狭い国家利益だけでものを考える時代はもはや過ぎ去ってしまった、という点を見てきました。それに代わって、いまやわれわれは国際協力、それに人類全体の安全と福利という立場で物事を見ていかなければならないのです。また国際化が、日本に固有な価値観の放棄や特色の喪失を意味するものでないこともはっきりしています。それどころか、国際化とは、より平和で安定も繁栄もしている世界のために日本が貢献できるように、いくつかの日本的特色を強化することを意味します。

　日本人がいま一つ変えなければならない考え方は、経済超大国の一員としての日本の国際的な地位を認識することです。日本人はもっと世界の諸問題についてしかるべき部分を引き受ける意欲を持つべきです。ということは、日本のもつ力や長所を他者と分かちあっていくことを意味します。この章で

means the sharing of Japan's strengths and good features with others. I should like to devote this chapter to a consideration of what some of Japan's particular strong points are and how Japanese should go about sharing them with other countries for their mutual benefit.

Looking back at history, we see that by the middle of the nineteenth century the long period of isolation under Tokugawa rule had left Japan technologically far behind the West. This made necessary a century of frantic scrambling to catch up. But this phase of history now lies in the past. Today Japan is abreast of the most advanced nations of the world in most matters and is probably the international leader in many. The other advanced industrialized countries now have at least as much to learn from Japan as it from them, and the less advanced nations find in Japan an admirable model of much of what they wish to learn. At this point in history, the internationalization of Japan means the spreading of Japan's achievements to other lands more than it means the traditional effort of the Japanese to catch up with the outside world.

私は、日本のとくに強い点のいくつかについて考え、日本人がどのようにしてそれらをお互いの利益のために他国と分かちあっていくべきかについて考えたく思います。

　歴史をふりかえって見ると、19世紀の中ごろの日本は、徳川政府の鎖国政策のために、技術面では西欧にずっとおくれをとっていました。そのために、１世紀にもわたり追いつくことを目指して狂おしいまでの努力がなされました。でも歴史のこの局面はもはや昔ばなしとなっています。いまや日本はほとんどの事項において世界の最先進諸国と肩を並べており、多くの分野においておそらくは世界を先導しています。いまでは日本が他の先進工業諸国から習うのと同じぐらいに、日本は彼らが習うに足るものを有しています。そして発展途上国は日本の中に、習うべき事項を多くもった仰ぐべき手本を見出しているのです。歴史の現時点における日本の国際化とは、いままでのように日本人が外部世界に追いつくべく努力を重ねるというよりは、日本が達成した業績を他の国々に波及していくことを意味しているのです。

Japanese Virtues

What are Japan's strong points that others may wish to copy? One outstanding Japanese virtue is the great capacity for cooperation within various groups and in modern times as a national unit. The way in which the Japanese in a single century moved without many violent domestic disturbances from a rigid feudal social and political system to an egalitarian and smoothly operating democracy is a remarkable achievement that deserves wide study and, where possible, emulation. That Japan is the only country of non-Western cultural background to have achieved an advanced democratic system, makes its experience of particular importance to the whole non-Western world.

Japan's skill at group cooperation in the field of modern industry is also of particular significance to the other advanced industrial nations, which for the most part, are having greater difficulties in this area. Instead of being the scene of clashes between owners and managers on the one side and workers on the other, as is the

日本人の美質

　では他者が真似たいと思っている日本の強い点とはどのようなものでしょうか。日本人の際立った美質の一つは、さまざまな集団の間で協力していける能力の大きさで、近年においてはそれは国家という単位の中での協力という形をとっています。わずか1世紀の間に、日本が国内で多くの荒々しい騒ぎもなしに、封建的でこちこちの社会的政治的なしくみから、平等主義の上に立ち円滑に機能している民主主義国家へと移行したのは、目を見はるような業績でして、広く検討され、可能なかぎり、模倣されるに値します。日本が非西欧の背景をもつ国としては唯一、高度の民主主義体制を達成したことにより、非西欧世界全体にとって日本の経験はとくに重要な意味をもつのです。

　近代産業という分野において日本がもつ集団協力の能力もまた、他の高度工業国家にとってとくに重要な意味をもっています。というのは、これらの国々の多くはいま、この分野においてたいへんな困難をかかえているからです。日本以外の地域においては、一方では企業のオーナーや経営者が、いま一方では労働者が陣どって、お互いに衝突するという光景

traditional pattern elsewhere, Japanese factories and businesses are organized more as joint communities of workers and managers, who cooperate smoothly together for the benefit of both, as well as for the benefit of the owners and the nation as a whole. This is a pattern that the countries of the West envy and seek to imitate in so far as they can in their own industrial systems.

Similarly the easy cooperation in Japan between business interests and the central government stands out as a most desirable alternative to the traditional attitudes in the West of rivalry and conflict between the two. The patterns Japan has achieved in relations between management and labor and between business interests and government are obviously more efficient and psychologically more satisfactory than the comparable patterns in the West. Fewer hours are lost in destructive strikes, workers have a greater sense of dignity and feel themselves to be full participants in their companies, and the economy as a whole can be more easily steered into productive channels. The modern Japanese economic system is generally recognized as having many features that the other advanced nations could usefully borrow, and it is one of the best overall

が昔からの形態を成してきました。ところが日本の工場や企業は、労働者と経営者の共同体といった形で組織され、お互いの利益、そしてオーナーや日本全体の利益のためになごやかに力を合わせて働くのです。この形態は西欧の国々にとっては羨ましいかぎりであり、自分たちの産業制度の中にできるだけとり入れようと努めています。

　同様に、経済界と中央政府との協力関係の気やすさは、両者の関係など、競争と葛藤のそれでしかないとする欧米流の伝統的な考え方の、きわめて望ましい代替案として、とくに際立っています。経営者と組合、企業と政府との関係において日本が作り出した形態も、欧米におけるそれと比べて、より効率が高く、心理的にも満足すべきものであることははっきりしています。破壊的な労働争議によって失われる労働時間は少なく、労働者が抱く自己への尊厳の念は高く、企業の完全な一員であると自覚し、全体としての経済も生産的な方向にもっていきやすい、というのが実体だからです。現在の日本の経済制度は、他の先進諸国が借用して役立たせることができる多くの特色を有する存在として広く認められており、工業的に開発途上にある国にとっては、そのあとを追うべき全般的形態として、最善なものの一つなのです。

patterns for the industrially less advanced countries to seek to follow.

Some other Japanese strong points go far back in Japan's culture. Examples are the willingness to work hard and the pride Japanese take in fine workmanship. These characteristics they probably derived from the ancient Confucian traditions of China and the whole of East Asia. As a consequence, they share these traits with their neighbors in China and Korea, but traditions of hard work and satisfaction in fine workmanship are not as common in many of the less developed countries. For these, the Japanese work ethic can be a very important inspiration.

Another characteristic that the Japanese share with the other lands with a Confucian cultural heritage is the great value they place on formal education and the unstinted efforts they expend on acquiring an education. In the complex modern world, high educational levels are a key to economic productivity and to success in many other areas as well. Japan today is unsurpassed in many fields of education, such as mathematics and engineering. It gets a higher proportion of its young people through the twelve years of elementary and secondary schooling than does any

　それ以外の日本の強い点は、日本文化のはるか昔にまでさかのぼります。懸命に働く意欲や、日本人が仕事のできばえに抱く誇りは、その例です。これらの特徴はおそらくは中国ならびに東アジア全体の儒教の古い伝統に由来するものと思われます。ですから、日本人はこれらの性向を近隣の中国や朝鮮の人々と分かちあっているわけですが、ただ勤勉や仕事のできばえに対する誇りの伝統は、途上国の多くでは日本におけるほど一般的ではありません。これらの国々にとって、日本の勤労倫理はとても重要な刺　激^{インスピレーション}たりえます。

　儒教の文化伝統をもつ他の国々と日本が共有しているいま一つの特色は、正規の教育に置く価値の大きさと、教育を手に入れるために費す努力のおしみなさです。複雑をきわめる現代世界にあって、高い教育水準は、経済面での生産性だけでなく、経済以外の領域においても成功への一つの鍵となります。今日の日本は、数学や技術など教育の多くの分野においてどこにもひけをとりません。12年間の初等教育や中等教育課程を終える若い人々の比率は世界のどの国よりも高く、高等教育課程に進学する若者の比率は、わずかにアメリカにおくれをとるだけです。

other nation and is topped only by the United States in the percentage that goes on to higher education.

There are, of course, some weaknesses in Japanese education. For example, the curriculum is overly standardized and rigid; there is too much emphasis on the passing of examinations rather than the acquisition of useful knowledge and habits of independent thought; and Japanese schools have shown themselves to be particularly inept in the teaching of foreign languages. But taken as a whole, Japan's educational system is one of its strongest points, possessing many features which the other advanced nations could adopt with benefit and providing an admirable general pattern for the less advanced countries.

One of Japan's finest characteristics is the orderliness of its society. This is to be seen in many aspects of life. Vast numbers of Japanese live packed together in their great cities, but with little violence or severe friction. The levels of crime of all sorts are relatively low when compared with most less developed or even advanced countries. Most people look upon the police as their friends and cooperate with them. They also follow regulations meticulously, even petty ones like the crossing of streets against traffic lights. The

　むろん日本の教育にも弱点はあります。たとえば、カリキュラムがあまりにも画一的で柔軟性に欠け、有益な知識や自主的な考え方を身につけることよりも試験に通ることに力点がおかれることなど、がその例です。それに日本の学校は、外国語の教育においてはとくに効率が悪いことをあらわにしています。でも全体として見ますと、日本の教育制度は日本のもっとも強い点の一つで、他の先進国が採用してプラスになるような多くの特色を含んでおり、途上国にとってはすばらしい一般的なわくぐみを提供してくれます。

　日本のもつもっともすぐれた特質の一つは、社会の秩序正しさです。この点は生活の多くの面において見ることができます。日本の大都市では多くの人々がひどく混み合った状態で暮らしているのですが、暴力やきびしい葛藤はほとんどありません。一切の犯罪の発生率は、途上国はもとより先進国と比べても比較的低いのです。ほとんどの日本人は警察を友人とみなし、協力をおしみません。日本人はまた規則を守るのに細心で、赤信号で道を横切らないというようなささいなものについてもそうです。国民の人権擁護に対する要求もきびしく、裁判所も公平さや寛大さの実現に努めます。礼儀正

public demands the strict observation of human rights, and the courts strive for fairness and leniency. The informal social rules of politeness are carefully observed, and one sees very little open rudeness or bickering. All in all, it would be hard to find another large and crowded land in which life, at least on the surface, is so well regulated and smooth as it is in Japan.

Japan's orderliness probably stems from various sources, but these cannot be ascertained with certainty. It grows in part out of the country's Confucian background, but a similar heritage did not help China and Korea overcome their violent internal disturbances in recent times. The strength of Japanese family ties also has probably been of help in giving stability to society, but many countries in which family solidarity is much stronger than it is in contemporary Japan are prone to lawlessness and violence. More important may be the long stability under Tokugawa rule, which taught the Japanese to expect to live according to fixed social and political norms in a stable rather than disorderly society. Also important is the extraordinary egalitarianism of Japan today. Compared with most other countries, both advanced and backward, Japan has very

しさといった非公式な社交上の規則もきちんと守られており、公然たる無礼や言い争いに出くわすことはまれです。いずれにせよ、混み合った大きな国で、たとえ表面的にではあっても、生活が日本ほどうまく規制され円滑にはこんでいる国を見つけ出すことはむずかしいのです。

　日本のもつ秩序正しさにはおそらくはさまざまな理由があるのでしょうが、それが何であるかはっきりと見定めることはできません。一つには日本の儒教的な背景がからみあっているのでしょうが、近年の中国や朝鮮では同様の儒教の伝統が国内での激烈な紛争を克服できなかったことも事実です。日本における家族のきずなの強さも、おそらくは社会の安定の度を加えるうえに役立ったでしょう。でも、いまの日本よりも家族の連帯がもっと強靭でありながら、無法や暴力がまかりとおっている国もたくさんあります。より重要な理由として徳川幕府の治政下での長期にわたる安定を数えることができます。決められた社会的政治的な規範に従って、無秩序な社会よりも安定した社会で生きるよう日本人に教えたからです。いま一つ重要なのは今日の日本における例を見ないほどの平等主義です。先進後進のいずれであるとを問わず他の国々と比べ、日本にはたいへんな（個人的な）富もありませんし、逆に多数の恵まれない人々から成る下層階級もありません。出世への主たる道程である教育は、すべての人々に開

75

little great wealth and no large underclass of underprivileged people. Education, which is the main path to advancement, is open to all. The system seems fair to most people, and, therefore, receives overwhelming support from the populace.

Japan's orderliness is a quality that is important for a world full of hatred and strife. Northern Ireland, Central America, South Africa, Lebanon and Israel, Iran, Sri Lanka, Cambodia and the Philippines may be exceptional cases, but high rates of crime and severe tensions, if not civil strife, characterize much of the world in a way that is almost unknown in Japan. If Japan could somehow impart its orderliness to other areas, it would be a great boon to the world indeed.

Moving to another field, we see that Japan's culture has many specific elements that have already enriched the United States and other parts of the West and could be of value to the whole world. More important than individual cultural features, however, is the whole Japanese attitude toward culture. People in Japan, even when living under crowded urban conditions, maintain a stronger aesthetic sense and love of natural beauty than is to be found in most parts of

放されています。社会全体はほとんどの人々にとって公平^{フェア}なものだと見られており、それだけに一般国民の圧倒的な支持を受けているのです。

　憎しみや紛争に満ち満ちている世界にとって、日本のもつ秩序正しさというのは、重要な資質です。北アイルランドや中米や南アフリカ、レバノンやイスラエル、イランやスリランカ、カンボジアやフィリピンなどは例外的な存在かもしれませんが、いまの世界は、よしんば内戦とまではいかずとも、高い犯罪発生率やきびしい緊張によって特徴づけられています。でも、これらは日本ではまったくといってよいほど無縁な存在です。もしも日本が自国の秩序正しさを他の地域に輸出しうる道がどうにかして開かれるとすれば、世界にとって大きなプラスになるのはたしかです。

　別の分野に目を転ずるなら、われわれは日本文化の具体的な要素の多くがすでにアメリカ合衆国や西欧の他の地域を豊かにしたことを知っており、それが世界全体にとっても価値をもちうると思います。でも個々の文化的特色よりももっと大切なのは、文化に対する日本人の態度です。たとえ都会の混雑した状況で生活している場合でも日本人は世界の多くの地域におけるよりは強い美意識と自然の美しさへの愛情を保ちつづけています。また芸術面での成果や、めいめいが文化的な趣味を通じ、個人としての自己表現欲を生かしている点

77

the world. They also are more successful than most other peoples in keeping alive a desire for individual self-expression through their artistic accomplishments and the cultivation of their own particular cultural hobbies. One sees this in the high levels of drawing skills among the average Japanese, their remarkable musical achievements and appreciation, and their widespread interest in composing poetry. Such cultural matters may not be as crucial to human survival as are abilities in economic organization and skills in technology and social and political matters, but they are important for the quality of life. Japan's contributions to the world in this area might prove no less important than its achievements in the more immediately evident economic, social, and political fields.

Problems in Giving Aid

I have suggested here merely a sampling of the various areas in which Japan can make a great contribution to the world. A more detailed consideration would provide sev-

において、他のほとんどの国民よりも成功しています。ふつうの日本人ですらが絵を描くことができ、実技と鑑賞の両面で音楽に通じ、詩作への関心が広範にわたっていることなどに、この辺の事情を見てとることができます。こういった文化的な事項は、人間の存立にとって、経済面での組織化能力や技術面での熟練、それに社会的政治的なことがらほど決定的な重要性をもっていないかもしれませんが、生活の風格^{クオリティ・オブ・ライフ}にとっては大切なことです。この分野での日本の貢献は、経済、社会、政治といった、だれの目にもより明らかな分野での成果にまさるとも劣らず重要であることがはっきりするかもしれません。

援助にあたっての問題点

　私は、日本が世界に対して大きな貢献をなしうるいくつかの分野について、限られた例をあげ素描をこころみてきました。いま少し詳細にわたってこの問題を考えれば、日本人が

eral scores or even hundreds of specific achievements and qualities the Japanese could with benefit share with their fellow men. But the problem remains how can this be done? The Bible says "It is more blessed to give than to receive," but it is also more difficult. It is not very easy to transfer attitudes and skills from one country to another except by the slow and uncertain method of setting an example.

In early times the Chinese and Koreans and more recently the countries of the West gave much to Japan, but they were able to do this only because the Japanese were eager to learn from them. Since World War II, the advanced nations have encountered frequent disappointments in their efforts to contribute to the less advanced lands and not infrequently have found their efforts did more harm than good. Some few countries, like Japan before them, will prove capable of learning on their own from Japan and the other advanced nations. South Korea, Taiwan, and Singapore come to mind as examples. But most countries will need great help even when they are eager to learn. The advanced nations will have to expend great efforts and acquire special skills in sharing their knowledge.

世界の同胞と分かちあい彼らに役立つ数十、いや数百もの具体的な成果や資質をあげることになりましょう。ただ問題は、それをどのようにして成し遂げるかにあります。新約聖書は「与うるは受くるよりも幸いなり」とうたっていますが、同時にそれはよりむずかしくもあるのです。考え方や技量を一国から他国に移そうと思えば、手本を示すという手間ひまのかかる、しかも不確かきわまりない方法による以外に、安易な道などないのです。

　初期においては中国人や朝鮮人が、そして近年に至っては欧米諸国が日本に多くを与えました。しかし、それとても日本人自身が受け入れに熱心だったればこそ可能だったのです。第二次大戦以降、先進諸国は発展途上諸国に対する貢献に努力しつつも、しばしばその過程で失望に出会い、途上諸国に対しプラスになるよりはむしろマイナスをもたらしていることに気づくのも、一度や二度ではありませんでした。かつての日本のように、2、3の国々は、日本などの先進諸国から自前でなにかを身につける能力があることを実証してみせるでしょう。韓国、台湾、シンガポールなどがその例としてあげることができます。でもほとんどの国々は、たとえ熱意があっても、多くの援助を必要とします。先進国の方がうんと努力して、自分たちの知識をどう共有していくかについての特別な技能を身につけなければなりません。

For Japan the easiest aspect of this task will be the providing of adequate finances. With a strong yen and a tremendously favorable balance in its trade and financial dealings with the rest of the world, Japan is almost surfeited with money. It also devotes only about one percent of its GNP to military defense, which is much less than any other major advanced nation and most less developed countries. It, therefore, has great leeway for a vastly increased aid program to bolster the security and stability of the world. There should be no difficulty for Japan's leaders and its people to earmark plenty of funds for worthy aid projects, which will contribute vastly more to Japan's own security and continued well-being than would battleships and military aircraft or a further expansion of its factories and exports.

The problem, however, is not primarily a budgetary one. It is more a matter of individual perceptions and of the willingness to make personal contributions of time and effort. Each of you must first understand what the problems are. Every thinking Japanese should know enough about his own culture and the cultures of other countries to realize what characteristics the Japanese have that could be of value to others. In other words, he must

　この責務のうち、日本にとっていちばんたやすいのは、十分な財政的な援助を提供することでしょう。円が強く、対外経済関係においても貿易収支面と資金勘定面の双方で大幅な黒字をかかえている日本は、お金がダブついているとすらいえます。しかも軍事面ではＧＮＰの１パーセント程度しか使っておらず、この点では他の主要先進国やほとんどの途上国をうんと下まわっています。ですから世界の安全と安定の強化のために、いまよりははるかに巨額の援助計画を実施するだけの大きな余地をもっているのです。日本の指導者と国民の双方にとって、有意義な援助計画にたくさんの資金を拠出することには何の困難もないはずです。軍艦や軍用機、もしくは工場や輸出をこれ以上ふやすよりも、よほど日本自体の安全と福利の継続に大きく寄与するでしょう。

　でも主たる問題は、予算をつけるという次元ではありません。一人一人のものの見方と、時間と労力の両面で個人が貢献する気持ちになるかどうかの方が問題なのです。まず第１に皆さんは何が問題なのかを理解しなければなりません。ものを思う日本人であればだれでも、自分自身と他の国々の文化について十分な知識をもつことによって、日本人のいくつもの特徴の中から、他者にとって価値があるのは何かをわきまえるべきです。ことばを変えていうなら、日本のもってい

have an appreciation of Japan's strong points and how these strong points might be usefully imitated by other countries. When Japanese attribute their virtues to certain unique, mystical traits, they are simply closing their minds and locking their doors against a useful participation in world affairs. When they flaunt their strong points with arrogance in the face of less successful countries, they kill the desire to learn on the part of those who need help. Either of these attitudes on the part of Japanese amounts to a sort of withdrawal into isolation, which under contemporary conditions would lead to the development of further imbalances in the world and ultimately a collapse of the global economic system, with resultant catastrophe for Japan itself.

Individual Effort

Each of you needs to study more carefully the good and bad points about the Japanese system and how these compare to the virtues and vices of other nations. You should

る強い点が何であり、どうしたらこれらの点を他の国々が有益な形で範としうるかを、理解してかかるべきなのです。日本人がもし自分たちの美質を、ある種の日本に固有な神秘的な性向に起因させるようでは、心を閉ざし、とびらに鍵をかけることになり、世界の動きに有益な形で参画していくことを、われとわが手で封ずることになってしまいます。また日本ほどの成功を収めていない国々を相手に、自分たちの長所を吹聴して歩くような尊大なことでは、助けを必要としている人々の（日本に）まねびたいという意欲を削ぐことになるでしょう。このような態度はいずれもが、日本人をある種の孤立へと内攻させることになり、それは今日の状況下にあっては、世界の不均衡を一層ひどいものにし、ひいては地球大での経済制度の崩壊をもたらし、その結果、日本自体も破局におちいることになってしまいます。

個々人の努力

皆さん一人一人は、制度としての日本についてその長所も短所も注意深く学び、それが他の国々の美質や悪徳と比べてどうであるかを検討すべきです。すべての国家的制度に通底

recognize the universalities of the problems underlying all national systems, the elements of the Japanese system that would be of most value to other countries, and the methods by which such features of the Japanese system can be adapted to and adopted by the multitude of very different countries in the world. All this calls for profound study of Japan as well as of other countries and an openness of mind both to existing differences and to the possibilities for new combinations of features.

Only after each of you individually has gained a greater understanding of the problems involved will you be ready to attempt to do something about them. At this point, we encounter the matter of will. People individually must be ready to devote time and effort to helping citizens of other countries learn what is most worth knowing about in Japanese society and culture. They also must be sensitive to the strong points of other countries, showing a reciprocal appreciation and willingness to learn from them. Even the most advanced countries will find things to admire and perhaps emulate even in the most backward countries.

している問題の普遍性を認識するとともに、システムとしての日本を構成する諸要素のうち、他国にとってももっとも価値のあるものは何であり、加えてこれらの諸要素を世界のきわめて多様な人々が適応し採用していくための方途が何であるかを認識する必要があります。そのためには他国だけでなく日本自体を突っこんで勉強するとともに、現存する相違や、さまざまな特色の新しい組み合わせの可能性について、広く心を開くことが求められます。

　皆さん一人一人がどのような問題点が関係しているのかについての知的理解を深めたのちにこそ、それへの対応を心がけることがはじめて可能となります。ここで個人の意志の問題に出会うことになるのです。一人一人の日本人が、他国の人々が日本の社会と文化について知るに値することがらを身につけられるように、自分の時間と労力を使って手助けする心がまえをもたねばなりません。同時に、他の国々の強い点についても鋭敏になり、彼らから習うという互恵的な精神や意志を見せなければなりません。もっとも先進的な国の場合でも、もっとも後進的な国の中にすら、感銘し、もって範とすべきいくつもの点を見出しうるのです。

Each of you individually can find opportunities to contribute to this learning process. But to do so will require a conscious effort to search them out. In my earlier chapter, I mentioned the importance of travel. More important would be longer residency abroad. Meaningful contacts with students from abroad or other foreign residents in Japan is an opportunity more possible for many of you and one of perhaps equal importance. By maximizing your contacts with foreigners of all kinds and making these more fruitful, you can individually participate in the exchange of knowledge and skills which is so important for the whole world at this time. You do not have to wait for the Japanese government to take the lead in programs of technological and cultural interchange, but can make a beginning on your own.

Official government effort, however, will in the long run be necessary if Japan is to make a serious attempt to play its appropriate role in the world in striving to head off chaos and achieve peace, stability, and prosperity for mankind as a whole. What sorts of programs should the Japanese government undertake? The most obvious and easiest to implement is financial and technological aid. But these require, besides money, a great deal of

　この学習過程に貢献する機会は、皆さん一人一人が見つけることができます。でもそのためには、それを追い求めるという、意識的な努力が要ります。第1章で私は旅行の意義について語りましたが、それよりももっと大事なのは、長期にわたって外国に住むことでしょう。また外国人の留学生や在日外国人との有意義な交流は、皆さんの多くにとってもっと手っとりばやい、しかしおそらくは同じくらいに重要な機会です。あらゆる種類の外国人との交流を最大限にふやし、それをより実りの多いものにしていくことで皆さんは、今日の世界にとって重要きわまりない知識と技能の行きかいに個人として参画できるのです。日本政府が、技術文化交流などで音頭をとるまで、徒らに待っている必要はないので、皆さん自身が自前でスタートを切れるのです。

　とはいうものの、全人類のために混乱（ケイオス）の可能性を未然に摘みとり、平和と安定と繁栄とを達成すべく、日本にふさわしい役割を演じていく上の真剣な努力を行なっていくためには、やはり公的機関による努力が長い目で見れば必要です。では日本政府は、どのような計画に手を染めるべきなのでしょうか。何よりも自明でしかも実施が容易なのは、経済ならびに技術面での援助です。しかし、お金以外にも、多くの知識と注意深い気くばりがないと、これはうまくいきません。日本

knowledge and careful thought to carry them out successfully. Japan must avoid programs which are designed more to increase its own export market than the economic growth and healthy independence of the recipient. In the past, Japanese aid programs have often been criticized for failing to meet this test.

Japan must also deal tactfully with the sensibilities of receiving nations. Aid recipients often desire showy projects, such as high-rise buildings, magnificent boulevards, steel mills, or international jet lines, which boost their pride but often are economically inappropriate for them. They need to be steered into more solid areas of less spectacular economic achievement, but this has to be done with great tact so as not to injure their self-esteem.

Difficult though these matters may be, the chief problem Japan will face in a major aid program will be the matter of personnel. Aid cannot be achieved simply by making money available. It is basically the transfer of skills between individual people. Foreign students coming to Japan will be part of the answer, but a bigger part will be the willingness of suitably trained Japanese to go abroad, often to remote areas under undesirable living conditions,

自体の輸出市場の拡大が先決で、援助を受ける側の経済成長
や健全な独立なんぞ二の次、という式の援助計画は避けるべ
きです。いままでの日本の対外援助は、この点で不合格だと
して、しばしば批判の対象になってきました。

　日本はまた援助を受ける国々の感受性ともうまく折れ合っ
ていくことが大切です。被援助国というのは、ややもすると
派手な見てくれの計画を望むものです。高層建築物とか、み
ごとな大通り<ruby>大通り<rt>ブルバード</rt></ruby>とか製鋼所とか、国際的な航空会社とかがこれ
で、いずれもその国民のプライドをくすぐりはしても、経済
的には不向きです。ですから見た目には派手でなくとも、も
っと堅実な分野に関心を向けるようにしていく必要がありま
す。ただし彼らの自尊心を損なうことのないよう、慎重な取
り扱いが肝心です。
　これらはみなむずかしいことではありますが、日本が大型
の援助計画で直面するであろう最大の問題は、人員にかかわ
るものです。ただ単にお金を出すだけでは援助の目的は達せ
られないのです。個人間における技能の移転、というのが援
助の本質なのです。日本への外国人留学生の招致というのは、
たしかにそれへの回答の一部ではありますが、もっと大きな
ものは、しかるべき訓練を受けた日本人が進んで海外に出か
け、それも望ましいとはいえない生活条件下の僻地もあえて

and their capacity to work effectively in unfamiliar and difficult circumstances. Japan, in short, needs a greatly expanded number of overseas volunteers, comparable in spirit but more effective in results than the American Peace Corps of earlier years.

One weakness of the whole Japanese system is its tendency to discriminate against individuals who leave the beaten track of career success in Japan and spend time abroad, especially in less developed countries. To this handicap is added the weakness of most Japanese in speaking an internationally used language, such as English. Less visible but probably more serious is the Japanese tendency to regard their own country as unique and to look down on other countries as being inferior. The Japanese abroad is noted for his clannishness, his disdain for the local culture, and his unhappiness over being in what he considers temporary banishment. A great deal must be done by individual Japanese to develop the right attitudes which will make them effective participants in truly successful aid efforts. This is basically a problem for you young Japanese, upon whom government programs will ultimately depend.

対象にして、不馴れかつ困難な状況のもとで成果を上げるような働きを示すことにあります。ひとことでいえば、日本が必要としているのは、一昔前のアメリカの平和部隊と精神においては匹敵しながらも、その結果においてはもっと大きな、海外向けのボランティアの人々をうんとふやすことなのです。

　日本の全体のしくみにおける一つの弱点は、日本での出世エリートコースを離れて、海外、それもとくに途上国で何年かを過ごす人々をとかく差別するという傾向です。この弱点に加え、ほとんどの日本人が、たとえば英語のような、国際的に使われていることばを話すことに弱い、という問題があります。いま一つ、それほど表には見えませんが、おそらくより深刻な点は、日本人がとかく自分たちの国のことを特異な存在とみなし、他国を劣っているとして見下す傾向があることです。海外在住の日本人は、自分たちだけでかたまり、土地の文化を軽蔑し、しばらくの間の島流しと思って鬱々として愉しまない、ことで知られています。ほんとうに効果の上がる援助活動の一員として成果を収めるためには、個々の日本人がしかるべき考え方を養っていかねばならず、多少の努力を払わねばならないでしょう。これは主として皆さんのような若い人々の問題なので、政府の計画といえども究極的には皆さん次第なのです。

As already mentioned, another major way in which Japan can contribute to the world is through formal education in Japan. Despite the excellence of Japan's educational system, the country has failed miserably in playing an international role in this field commensurate with its international standing. In the United States and most of the other advanced countries, universities are full of students, researchers, and even professors from less developed countries as well as the other advanced nations. In Japan, in contrast, there are virtually no foreign students, research workers, or teachers, except for a sprinkling in special programs or with special status. Japan is obviously losing the opportunity to profit from contact with large numbers of foreign scholars and students and failing to live up to its duty to make its superb educational system contribute to the welfare of the world as a whole.

Overcoming the Educational Barrier

Two barriers stand in the way of Japan playing its proper educational role. The first is psychological. Japan has

　すでに申しましたように、日本が世界に寄与できるいま一つの主な方法は、日本の学校教育を通じてです。日本の教育制度はたしかにすぐれてはいるのですが、日本はその国際的な立場にふさわしい役割をこの分野で果たすことに、みじめなまでに失敗してきました。アメリカであれ他の先進諸国の大半であれ、大学というのは他の先進国や開発途上国からの学生や研究者、そして教授をすら大勢かかえています。ところがそれとはうらはらに日本では、特殊な課程か、特別な地位のごくごく少数を例外として、外国人の学生や研究者や教官は、皆無にひとしいのです。多数の外国の学者や学生と接触することを通じてプラスを得ることのできる機会を失い、その最高の教育制度を、全世界の福利のために役立たせるという義務を怠っている日本、といえるように思います。

教育面での障害を乗り越える

　日本が教育の分野でしかるべき役割を演ずることを妨げている障害には2つあります。その第1は心理的なものです。

created for itself a narrow, exclusive educational system, which in effect confines most Japanese to a restricted, uniform educational experience and excludes virtually all outsiders. The Japanese need to realize the desirability—one might better say, necessity—of a broader more diverse educational system in this age of global interdependence. How is this to be achieved? Individual young Japanese also should expand their own educational experiences by learning more about other peoples and what they are thinking. They and others also should influence the government to see education in a broader light that encourages greater diversity and a more international point of view.

But this still leaves the other and greater barrier—the problem of language. There are extremely few foreign students who already know enough Japanese to be able to profit from the Japanese educational system and not many who are willing to take the time to acquire the necessary mastery of it. They wonder why they should devote years to this arduous task only to find they have little use for Japanese after completing their education. Even the Japanese find it necessary to learn some international language, such as English, to conduct most of their business

日本は自国のために、狭くて非開放的な教育制度を作り上げることで、事実上ほとんどの日本人に制約の多い画一的な教育体験を押しつけ、外部者のほとんど一切を排除してきました。でも今日のような地球大での相互依存時代においては、より広範で、もっと多様性に富んだ教育制度が望ましい、いや欠かせない、ということに気づかなければなりません。ではこれをどのようにして達成したらよいのでしょうか。個々の若い日本人も、他の国民や彼らが何を考えているかについてもっと勉強することで、自分たちの教育体験を拡げていくことが必要です。若い人々も他の人々と力を合わせてより多くの多様性と、より多くの国際的な視点を進めていけるように、そして教育をもっと広い立場から見るように、政府に影響をあたえていくべきでしょう。

でもそこまで行ったとしても、いま一つの、より大きな障害は残りつづけます。ことばの壁がそれです。すでに充分な日本語を身につけ、日本の教育制度から何かを得ることのできる外国人学生はごく少数ですし、そのために必要な日本語をものにすべく時間をかけることを煩わない外国人学生も、そう数多くはありません。教育課程を終わってからはあまり実際に使うことがないとわかっているのに、なぜ日本語の習得というたいへんな仕事に長い年月をかけなければならないのか、というのが彼らの気持ちなのです。日本人ですら、経済活動の大半を海外で行なったり、科学技術の分野での国際社会に参加していくためには、たとえば英語のような、国際

activities abroad or to participate in the international world of science and technology. Would it not make better sense, the foreign student feels, to study in a country where the language is already somewhat familiar to him and will serve him better in later life as a language of international communication? Thinking in this way, foreign students flock to America or Europe, rather than Japan, and the few who do come to Japan, lured largely by financial grants, are likely to be disappointed by the slowness of their progress and repelled by the exclusiveness of Japanese society.

There obviously is need for major changes in Japan if it is to play the educational role required of it in the present day. Even the large numbers of Japanese children who are now being raised in part abroad require special arrangements. They return to Japan with a firm grasp of some foreign language, usually one of broad international usage, but then are virtually forced to abandon their start in this language and their understanding of the attitudes of a foreign country in order to catch up in the difficult Japanese writing system and learn the attitudes taught in the narrow Japanese approach to education. They are brainwashed

語のどれかを身につけねばならないと思っているのです。そ
れなら、と外国人留学生は考えるのです。そのことばがすで
に多少はわかっていて、しかもあとになって国際的な意思伝
達の手段としてもっと役に立つようなことばをもった国で勉
強する方が理にかなっているではないか……。このように考
えて外国人留学生は日本よりは、合衆国やヨーロッパへとひ
しめくように向かうのです。そして、たまたま日本を選んだ
少数の留学生——奨学資金などに惹かれてのことが多いので
すが——も自分たちの進歩のおそさにがっかりし、日本社会
の排他性に反撥することが多いのです。

　今日において求められている教育面での役割をもし日本が
果たしていこうとするなら、日本自身が大幅な変化を必要と
しているのは明白です。若い時代の一部を海外で過ごしてい
る多数の日本人の子弟にも、特別な取り決めが必要とされま
す。彼らは何らかの外国語をしっかりと身につけて帰国しま
す。だいたいが広範に使われている国際語のどれかであるこ
とが多いのですが、そのことばにおけるせっかくの利点や外
国人の考え方についての理解は事実上捨て去ることを強制さ
れる、といっても過言ではありません。さもないと、むずか
しい日本の表記法に追いつき、日本式の狭い教育理念で教え
こまれる考え方がものにならないからです。いわば洗脳され
るといってもよく、かくして彼らはせっかく、海外で育った

in a way and lose much of the special value they acquired through growing up abroad. Japan, which is much in need of their knowledge of foreign languages and psychology, thoughtlessly casts away these potential pearls in its insistence on making the product of its educational system a gravel of uniform size and quality.

Three things of great value to Japan could be achieved if it were to broaden its educational system to include a second track that has a wider, international curriculum and utilizes a foreign language in part for education. Through such a system, Japan could preserve among its children raised abroad the foreign language skills and international attitudes that are desperately needed for Japan's own survival in the present world. It would also attract large numbers of foreign students, especially from the less developed nations. This in turn would make it possible for Japanese, not only to broaden their own outlook and international experience, but also contribute much more than they now do to the world.

If an international track were set up by some of the most prestigious universities, such as Tokyo University, it would soon be crowded with applicants, because Japa-

ことによって身につけた特別な価値のほとんどを喪失してしまう、ということになります。外国語や外国人の心理についての彼らの理解をうんと必要としている日本でありながら、これらの潜在的な「珠玉」を無思慮にも投げ捨ててしまっている、というわけで、これもその教育制度を一律的な大きさと質をもった有無をいわさぬ教壇用の木槌に仕立てようと計ればこその損失なのです。

もしも日本がその教育制度をもう少し幅の広いものに切りかえ、より広範で、国際的なカリキュラムを組み、教育用語に外国語を一部使うようにするという、いまとはちがった第2の路線を含むようになれば、3つの大きな価値をもった成果の達成が可能です。このような制度を通じ日本は、海外帰国子女のせっかくの外国語の技能や国際的な考え方を温存することができます。それらは今日の世界にあって生き抜いていく上に、日本が絶対に必要としているものなのです。またこのような制度は、海外、なかでも発展途上国からの留学生を多数ひきつけることになるでしょう。そうすれば、日本人自身がその理解や国際的体験を拡げるだけでなく、いま以上の世界への貢献を可能にするでしょう。

もしも国際的な「路線」が、東京大学のような有力大学のいくつかに設けられるということになれば、すぐに志願者が殺到することになりましょう。というのは、日本の経済界や

nese business and intellectual leaders would see that its products were often of more use to them than the graduates of the more traditional, purely Japanese track. It would also attract large numbers of foreign students, researchers, and teachers, who would not only help bring true internationalization to Japan, but would also serve as a major channel for the dissemination of Japan's strong points to the rest of the world. In these ways, it would be a major contribution to world peace and prosperity as well as the continued wellbeing of Japan itself.

One should not forget, however, that behind such efforts in education and international aid lies the necessity of having the right attitudes. Japanese must wish strongly to internationalize their own thinking and accept foreigners into their own society with kindness and goodwill. They must see that in this way, they themselves will learn to live smoothly with the other peoples of the world.

Here we return to the attitudes of individuals. Each one of you can make a vital contribution by learning how best to contribute to the development of such attitudes and by putting them into practice when the opportunity offers. Japan is a great nation today that has much to

知的世界の指導者が、より伝統的で純粋に日本的な「路線」よりは、この新型「路線」の卒業生のほうが、よほど役に立つ、ということに気づくだろうからです。外国からの留学生や研究者、さらには教育者も多数ひきつけることになり、単に真の国際化を日本にもたらすことにとどまらず、日本の強い点を広く海外に伝播するための主要な媒体として機能することになるでしょう。こうしたことを通じて世界の平和や繁栄だけではなく、日本自体の福利の継続にも大きな貢献となります。

　ただ一つ、教育や対外援助面での努力の背後には、正しい考え方がなければならないことを忘れるべきではありません。日本人が自分たちの考えを国際化したいと強く望み、外国人を自分たちの社会に、親切と善意とをもって受け入れていかなければなりません。こうしてこそ、世界の他の人々と平穏に共存していくことを身につけられると悟るべきです。

　またしてもここで個人の考え方に立ち戻ることになります。皆さん一人一人は、このような考え方の涵養に寄与するにはどうしたらいちばんよいかを身につけ、機会あるごとにそれを実践に移していくことで、貴重な貢献をすることができます。今日の日本は偉大な国の一員であり、世界に提供できる

offer the world. But the effort must start with the individual. It is people like yourself who first must learn more about your country and other lands and then develop the understanding and will to contribute personally in so far as your circumstances permit to the transfer of desirable Japanese knowledge and skills to other lands and the development of goodwill and cooperation between Japan and the outside world. Only if individual Japanese do this and the government follows with comprehensive and wise policies can we look to the future of the world, including Japan, with a certain degree of optimism.

ものも多いのです。でもそのための努力は、まず個人に発し
なければなりません。まず最初に自分の国や他国についても
っと多くを知り、ついで理解を増進し、そして、望ましい日
本のもつ知識や技能を他国に伝え、日本と外部世界との善意
と協力との促進のために、事情の許すかぎり個人として貢献
していくべきなのは、皆さんのような人々なのです。日本人
一人一人がこれを手がけ、そのあとを政府が包括的かつ賢明
な政策で後追いしていくということになったときにはじめて、
私たちは日本をはじめとする世界の未来を、多少の楽観論と
ともにのぞきみることができるのです。

On Studying a Foreign Language
外国語を習うことについて

CHAPTER 3

On Studying a Foreign Language

In my previous chapters on world citizenship and some of the strong points in Japanese culture, I mentioned the study of foreign languages several times as being a matter of great importance. It is, in fact, such a vital subject that it deserves a whole chapter devoted just to it.

Next to their isolationist attitude of feeling themselves to be unique, the special difficulty the Japanese have in learning foreign languages is probably the greatest barrier standing in the way of their making the contributions they should to world peace and stability. This difficulty has made Japan relatively silent in international councils, causing people to describe it as being like a mute giant or the big boy who tries to remain unnoticed in the back of the classroom. Charles de Gaulle is said to have once described Prime Minister Hayato Ikeda as being like a "transistor salesman" in his inability to discuss world affairs. The language barrier has certainly made Japan less influential

第3章

外国語を習うことについて

　地球市民と、日本文化の長所のいくつかに関するこれまでの2つの章で、私はごくごく大切なことがらの一つとして、外国語の学習について何度か触れました。実はこのテーマ、きわめて重要ですので、それだけで1章を設ける価値があります。

　自分たちがユニークだとする孤絶感について、外国語学習にあたって日本人が直面する困難は、世界の平和と安定とに対し日本人が行なってしかるべき貢献の前に立ちはだかる最大の障壁といえます。この困難は日本をして国際的な討議の場であまり発言させないようにしむけ、日本をものいわぬ巨人とか、教室のうしろの方でできるだけ人目につかぬように身を縮めている少年、と呼ばせるに至ったのです。シャルル・ドゴール（元フランス大統領）は池田勇人首相（当時）のことを「トランジスターのセールスマン」呼ばわりをしたといわれていますが、それは池田氏が国際問題を議論することができなかった故でした。ことばの障壁のために、日本がその経済的大きさにふさわしい影響力をふるうことができなかったのは確かで、他国との関係を必要以上によそよそしいも

than its economic size would warrant. It has also made its relations with other countries less friendly than they could be. In this way, it has damaged the security and wellbeing of Japan itself. The learning of foreign languages may seem to some people a relatively minor matter, but certainly in Japan's case it is a problem of major concern.

International relations, which have become so important these days, require a common language for the exchange of ideas. Without one, misunderstandings easily arise and can lead to serious consequences. It is a pity that the Japanese, who lay such emphasis on understanding and consensus among each other, are so poorly equipped to achieve a similar degree of understanding and consensus with others. Their linguistic inabilities make them clumsy at explaining themselves to others and equally unable to understand another person's point of view. Simple translation is not enough, because nuances and sometimes the main point itself may be lost in translation. A free and easy give and take is required if true understanding is to be achieved.

In the field of business, Japanese have realized the absolute necessity of having sufficient language skills for

のにしたのも、このためでした。このように、日本自体の安全と福利にヒビを入れてきたのです。外国語の学習なんて、どちらかといえばささいなこととみなす人もいるでしょうが、日本の場合についていうなら、主たる関心事であることはまちがいありません。

　今日、国際関係はまことに重要なものとなったわけですが、それには、意思の交換のための共通の言語を必要とします。それがないと、容易に誤解が生まれ、それが深刻な結果を招来しかねません。自分たちの間の理解や意見の一致にあれほどの力点をおく日本人が、他者との間に同レベルの理解と意見の一致を達成するうえに、これほど恵まれていないのは、残念なことです。言語面での能力不足が、他者に対して自分を説明することをぎこちなくし、あわせて他者の見方を理解できなくしているのです。単なる翻訳では十分でありません。というのはニュアンスはもちろん、ときとしては主な論点そのものが翻訳の過程で失われてしまうからです。真の理解を達成するためには、自由で気のおけないやりとりが必要とされるのです。

　ビズネスの分野において、不足なく意思疎通していくためには、十分な言語上の技能が絶対に必要だということを日本

adequate communication, but they still lag behind other nations even in this area. The same could be said of science and technology and to some extent even the field of culture, though fortunately appreciation and understanding can transcend the language barrier in at least some aspects of culture. Still, in this age of international interdependence in which all nations must learn to cooperate peacefully with one another, full and easy understanding is necessary in all fields. This depends in turn on broad skills at communication, which in turn depend on language. Mastery of a common language of communication is a necessary foundation stone for the creation of any structure of international order and world peace. It also underlies our own individual effectiveness in participating in this important work.

Japanese Problems in Learning a Foreign Language

The question naturally arises why Japanese have special difficulties in learning foreign languages and thus face a

人は認識してきましたが、この領域においてすら日本人はいまだに他国におくれをとっています。同じことは科学や技術についてもいえるでしょうし、ある程度までは文化についても同じことがいえます。もっとも幸いなことに、いくつかの文化的側面についてだけは、鑑賞能力や理解はことばの障壁を乗り越えることができます。とはいえ、すべての国民がお互いに協力していくことを身につけねばならない国際的な相互依存の今日にあっては、すべての分野において十分かつたやすく理解していくことが必要です。ということは、意思伝達における広範な技能に依存せざるをえず、それはすなわちことばに依存するということになります。意思疎通のための共通言語をマスターすることは、国際的な秩序や世界平和のための構造をいかなるものであれ構築していく際の礎石として欠かせません。それはまたこの重要な仕事に参画していくにあたって、われわれ一人一人がどこまで有効でありうるかを決めてしまうのです。

外国語の習得にあたっての日本的な問題点

　それではなぜ日本が外国語を学習する際に特異な困難をかかえ、したがってとりわけ深刻な問題に直面しているのか、

particularly serious problem. People are often surprised to find at international conferences that the Japanese, because of their weakness in foreign languages, are among the least competent participants. Frequently they are the worst. A combination of factors probably explains this unhappy situation.

One, ironically enough, is the very advancement of Japanese culture. In many countries, education has not been developed enough to offer advanced instruction in all fields and publishing is not sufficiently advanced to produce enough books and periodicals of high quality in a country's own language. Young people are therefore forced to master a foreign language in order to gain an adequate education in many fields or to stay abreast of progress in them. Sometimes foreign languages are necessary for all advanced study or to conduct complicated economic and political affairs. A foreign language is often the lingua franca for a country made up of many tribes each with its own language or dialect. Even advanced nations of Western background, if they happen to be small, frequently find it necessary to utilize foreign languages for many purposes. A Danish scholar, for instance, will find it more sensible

という疑問が当然出てきます。国際会議の際に日本人は外国
語に弱いため、一番有能さに欠ける参加者の中に数えられる
ことを知って驚くこともしばしばです。いや、最悪のことも
しょっちゅうなのです。このような情けない状態の背景には、
おそらくはいくつかの要素が組み合わさっています。

　一つは、まことに皮肉なことながら、日本文化が高度に発
達しているという、まさにその理由です。多くの国々におい
ては、あらゆる分野で高等な教育をさずけるほど進んではお
らず、その国のことばで高水準の書籍や刊行物を出すほど出
版も進んではいないのです。したがって若い人は外国語の習
得を余儀なくされ、そうすることで十分な教育を身につけ、
進歩におくれをとるまいと努めており、これは多くの分野に
あてはまります。高等な学術研究と名のつくもののすべてや、
経済や政治の複雑なことがらをとり行なっていくうえに、外
国語が欠かせないこともままあるのです。またそれぞれの部
族語や方言をもつ多くの部族から成り立っている国において
は、ある外国語が共通語の役割を演ずることもしばしばです。
西洋の背景をもつ進んだ国ですら、その国が小さい場合には、
外国語を使っていろいろな用を弁じていくことが欠かせませ
ん。たとえば、デンマーク人の学者にとっては、世界を相手
にものをいおうと思えば、英語で発表するほうが、限られた
数の同国人相手にデンマーク語で発表するよりも気がきいて

to publish in English for a world audience rather than in Danish for a limited number of fellow Danes.

Japan is, of course, in a different position. Even the most advanced specialties can be studied in Japanese; almost all works of wide significance are translated into the language; and a huge reading public awaits books published in Japanese. It is not necessary for a Japanese to master a foreign language to pursue almost any advanced line of study or conduct complicated affairs, except for foreign trade. As a consequence, foreign language study becomes only a peripheral aspect of education, as it is in the English speaking countries. Where a statesman, businessman, or scholar attending an international conference from a less developed country or a small advanced one is very likely to have gained considerable competence in English or some other international language, a corresponding Japanese, even though possibly much more sophisticated and knowledgeable, may not feel at ease in any foreign language. He may be like the native English-speakers at the conference in his capacity to handle with skill only his own language. But there is one big difference. The native English-speaker can use his own language and therefore speaks with confi-

いる、ということになるのです。

　日本がちがった立場にあることは、いうまでもありません。
もっとも高度な専門研究でも日本語で可能ですし、広範な意
義をもつ作品はほとんどすべてが日本語に訳出されています。
それに巨大な読書人口が日本語で刊行される書籍を待ってい
ます。ほとんどの分野で高度な研究を進め、複雑なことがら
をとり行なっていくにあたり、貿易だけを唯一の例外として、
外国語をマスターすることは日本人には必要でないのです。
その結果、外国語の学習は、英語国の場合と同じく、教育の
中で周辺的な存在になってしまいました。途上国や小さな先
進国から国際会議に出てくる人が、政治家、実業家、学者の
別なしに、英語もしくは他の国際語について相当程度の熟練
を身につけていることが多いのに比べ、見識や知識の面にお
いてはあるいはもっと進んでいるかもしれないにもかかわら
ず、外国語となると何語であれ逃げ腰、というのが日本側参
加者なのです。自在に操れるのは母語だけ、という点で英語
国からの出席者と似ているといえましょう。ただここには大
きな違いがあります。英語を母語とする人は自分のことばを
使えばいいわけですから自信をもって話すことができます。
それに反し日本人は、通訳者にたよるか、ブロークン・イン
グリッシュにたよるかせねばならず、その結果、不明晰かつ
事情不案内、という風に見えてしまうのです。自分の思いを

dence. The Japanese, however, may have to resort to translators or to broken English, appearing as a result inarticulate and ill informed. He will be unable to communicate his thought clearly to others or comprehend fully what they are saying.

Another reason for the poor showing of Japanese as students of foreign languages is the relative poverty of the Japanese phonetic system. This situation forces the Japanese to face more unfamiliar sounds in learning a foreign language than is the case for most other peoples. The endless confusion of *l* and *r* is a good case in point. (Japanese lacks any real *l*.) The simple word "the" is likely to be pronounced *za*, constituting two serious phonetic mistakes. The common trade name "Brother," pronounced *Buraza*, contains at least four major phonetic errors. Consonant clusters and syllabic endings, as in "craft," "dog," or "cat," are unpronounceable to untutored Japanese. Few languages are phonetically so simple as Japanese and therefore raise so many problems in the learning of a foreign language.

Although huge numbers of names and words have been borrowed in the past into Japanese from Chinese and more recently from English, they are all pronounced by Japanese

相手に明確に伝えることもできなければ、相手のいうことを
十二分に理解することもできないのです。

　日本人が外国語の習得に得手でいないようにみえるいま一
つの理由として、日本語の音声システムがどちらかというと
貧弱なことがあげられます。この結果、他の言語を話す人々
と比べて、日本人が外国語学習の際に出くわす不馴れな音声
が多いという状況が生まれます。*l* と *r* との不断の混同は
この点をよく示しています。（日本語には本当の *l* 音は一つ
もないのです。）ごく簡単な the は za と発音され、2 つも
の深刻な音声上のあやまりを構成します。よくある商標の
Brother は Buraza と発音され、これまた少なくとも 4 つ
の音声上のあやまりを含みます。craft や dog や cat など
の、子音群集合や音節語尾は、事前に習ったことのない日本
人には発音不能です。他にあまり類例がないほど音声的に単
純なだけあって、日本語ということばは外国語の学習にあた
り多くの問題を引きおこすのです。

　また、昔は中国語、かつ最近では英語からたくさんの名前
や単語を借り入れたにもかかわらず、それがすべて日本人に
よっていかにも日本的に発音されるために、中国語や英語を

in a distinctively Japanese way that makes them usually quite unrecognizable to native speakers of Chinese or English. For example, the great Chinese leader Mao Zedong comes out as Mo Takuto in Japanese. The same situation exists with Korean names. The well-known Korean statesman Kim Daejung is rendered by the Japanese as Kin Daichu. In the case of English, borrowed words are not only grossly mispronounced but often develop new meanings or abbreviations. The English word "strike" is pronounced *sutoraiki* and is commonly abbreviated to *suto* when referring to a labor dispute, but it is pronounced *sutoraiku* and is never abbreviated when referring to the term in baseball. Japanese often become so accustomed to these standard mispronunciations of English words and their distorted meanings that they will use them even when speaking otherwise quite creditable English. It is quite confusing when Japanese use *handoru*, derived from "handle," to mean the "steering wheel" of a car or convert the one syllable name of the French writer Sartre into the four syllable monstrosity, *Sarutoru*.

母語とする人々には、まったく聞きとれないことがほとんど、という事実があります。たとえば、中国の偉大な指導者の毛沢東^{マオ・ツェ・トン}は、日本語ではモウタクトウと発音されます。朝鮮語の人名についても同じような状態が存在します。高名な韓国の政治家の金大中^{キム・デ・ジュン}が、日本語ではキンダイチューと発音されるという具合にです。英語からの借用語の場合は、すさまじく訛った形で発音されるだけでなく、新しい意味が生まれたり、略語化されることもしばしばです。英語の strike はストライキと発音され、労働争議を指すときにはストと略されるのが普通ですが、野球用語としてはストライクと発音され、しかも略されることは絶対にありません。日本人は英単語のこの種の「標準化された^{スタンダード}」訛った発音やねじ曲げられた意味にすっかり馴れっこになり、一応はそこらぞこらな英語をしゃべっているときでも、つい使ってしまうことがよくあるのです。自動車の「操舵輪^{ステアリング・ホイール}」のことを英語の handle をもとにハンドルと呼んでみたり、もともとは1シラブルの Sartre というフランスの作家の名前を、サルトルなどと4音節^{シラブル}の化け物同然に変身させてみたりするのです。

Japan's Linguistic Isolation

The chief problem for Japanese learning most foreign languages, however, is the fact that Japanese is a very different type of language from those spoken by most of the other peoples of the world. It belongs to a relatively small linguistic group called Altaic, lying in a broken band all the way across Asia and including Korean, Mongolian, and Turkish. Of these peoples, only the Koreans are in close contact with the Japanese, and the Turks, the next largest linguistic group, live largely at the western end of Asia, far removed from Japan.

In contrast to the loosely spread out and not very numerous speakers of the Altaic languages, the Indo-European family of languages occupies in thick clusters most of the world. Almost all of the people of the Western Hemisphere are speakers of English, Spanish, Portuguese, French, and Dutch—all Indo-European languages. The family covers virtually all of Europe, with the exception of the Hungarians, Finns, Estonians, Lapps and Basques, which are all

日本の言語的孤立

　でも、ほとんどの外国語を学習している日本人にとっての主たる問題は、日本語ということばが世界のほとんどの国民によって話されていることばとは、とても違ったタイプのものである、という事実です。日本語は、アルタイ語系という、比較的小さな語族に属しています。この語族、アジアを横切る形で切れ切れの帯状に横たわっており、朝鮮語、モンゴール語、それにトルコ語が含まれます。これらの人々のうち、日本人と密接なかかわりのあるのは朝鮮人だけで、それに次ぐ大きさをもつ言語集団のトルコ人は、その多くがアジアの西端に、日本人とははるかに離れた形で、居住しています。

　アルタイ語系の諸言語の話し手がまばらな形で拡がり、しかも多数でないのとは対照的に、インド・ヨーロッパ語族に属する諸言語は、世界の各地を、重なりあうようにして占めています。西半球のほとんどの諸国民は、英語、スペイン語、ポルトガル語、フランス語、オランダ語など、いずれもインド・ヨーロッパ語族の諸言語を話す人々です。この語族は全ヨーロッパをほとんどカバーしており、ハンガリー人やフィンランド人、エストニア人やラップ人、それにバスク人などの例外はあるにもせよ、これらはいずれもごくごく小さな集

very small groups. It spreads throughout much of Asia, including virtually all of Siberia, Iran, Afghanistan, Pakistan, Nepal, Sri Lanka, Singapore and most of the great population of India. It extends into parts of South Africa and is the language of the whole continent of Australia.

The only other linguistic group of comparable size is Sinitic, or the Chinese type of languages. A very solid block of high population, it embraces the various forms of Chinese and also Tibetan, Burmese, Vietnamese, Thai, and a number of tribal languages in Southeast Asia. Other relatively large language groups are Semitic in the Middle East and North Africa and Malayo-Polynesian, which spreads from the islands of the Pacific through the Philippines, through Indonesia and Malaysia to Madagascar off the coast of Africa. None of these other great families of languages are related in any fundamental way to Japanese and all are based on entirely different principles of organization. The Altaic languages stand out in unusual linguistic isolation, and they are very much less closely related to each other than are many of the languages in the other linguistic families. There is, for example, a much larger gulf even between Japanese and Korean than between English and German or French and Italian.

団なのです。この語族はシベリアのすべて、イラン、アフガニスタンにパキスタン、ネパールにスリランカ、シンガポールにインドの大人口のほとんどに及んでいます。南アフリカの各地域にも拡がり、オーストラリア全大陸のことばにもなっています。

　インド・ヨーロッパ語族に匹敵する大言語集団としては、シナ語族、つまりは中国語式の諸言語があるだけです。高い人口をもつ密度の濃いこの語族は、中国語のさまざまな形以外にも、チベット、ビルマ、ヴェトナム、タイ、の諸語と、東南アジアのいくつもの部族語を包含しています。そのほかに、相当の大きさをもつ語族は中近東ならびに北アフリカのセム語族とインドネシアとマレーシア、そしてフィリピンを経て太平洋の島々からアフリカ大陸沖のマダガスカルにまで展開しているマレー・ポリネシアン語族、をあげることができます。これらの主要語族のどれをとってみても、日本語と基本的なところでつながっているものはなく、いずれもまったくちがう組織原理の上に成り立っています。アルタイ語系の諸言語はまれにみるほどの言語的な孤立という点で際立っており、他の語族の多くの言語と比べても、お互い同士の関連性はきわめて少ないのです。たとえば日本語と朝鮮語との間の差異は、英語とフランス語、ドイツ語とイタリア語のそれよりもぐんと大きいのです。

Japan's linguistic isolation is underscored by its unique writing system, which is one of the most difficult in common use anywhere in the world. It does share with the countries of East Asia the horrendously complex writing system of a few thousand unique Chinese characters, but even this unity is being lost. The Chinese are modifying their characters in one direction and the Japanese in another, while the Koreans and Taiwanese use the original characters unchanged. In Japan, Chinese characters are being increasingly supplanted by two different types of phonetic syllabaries, while in Korea the excellent Korean phonetic system of hangul is rapidly overspreading the entire use of Chinese characters. At an earlier time, Latin letters replaced characters completely in Vietnam.

Since the Japanese have a very distinctive type of language and an extraordinarily complex writing system, it is not surprising that they find it difficult to learn most foreign languages or that few foreigners, except for Koreans, find it easy to master Japanese. With the exception of Korea, the various peoples with whom the Japanese have had most contact throughout history have all spoken very different types of language from Japanese. The

　日本の言語的孤立はそのユニークな表記法によってさらに強調されています。普通に使われている表記法の中で、世界のどこに行ってもこれほどむずかしいものはそうありません。たしかに東アジアの諸国と、数千のユニークな漢字から成る、複雑きわまりない表記法を共有してはいますが、この一致ですらがいまでは失われつつあります。中国大陸では漢字をある方向で簡素化しつつあるのに反し、朝鮮民族や台湾の中国人は従来どおりの漢字をそのまま使っています。日本では漢字はますます平仮名と片仮名という表音式の表記法にとってかわられつつあります。他方、朝鮮ではハングル文字というすぐれた表音表記法が、急速に全面的な漢字の使用を追いやりつつあります。ヴェトナムではもっと早い時期にラテン文字が漢字に完全に代替しています。

　日本語がきわめて際立っていることと、表記法が異常なまでに複雑なことを思うと、日本人がほとんどの外国語の習得に困難を覚え、朝鮮人を除いて日本語をマスターすることを容易と思っている外国人が少ないのも驚くにはあたりません。朝鮮を例外として、日本人が歴史を通じいちばん交流をもってきたさまざまな民族は、日本語とはひどく違ったことばをしゃべる人々でした。中国人のことばは日本語とは似ても似つかぬことばです。日本が重要なかかわりを展開してきたインド・ヨーロッパ語族のことばのさまざまな話し手について

127

Chinese have a radically different tongue. So also do the various speakers of Indo-European languages with whom Japan developed important contacts. These include the Indians, from whom the Japanese learned Buddhism; the Portuguese, Spanish, Dutch, and English, who appeared on their shores in the sixteenth and seventeenth centuries; and the Americans, Russians, French, and Germans, who came in later years.

The reasons why Japanese find it difficult to learn other languages serve in reverse to explain why their language is not likely to become a great international tongue. It and its difficult writing system are simply too hard for others to learn. True international languages are a fairly modern development, though great regional languages have existed for some time. Latin was a regional language throughout the Roman Empire and continued as such in written form in parts of the West until recent centuries. Written Chinese had a much longer role as the international language of East Asia. Arabic served the same purpose for a while for much of the Middle East, North Africa, and parts of Europe. Even Mongolian and Turkish had brief moments in history as regional languages.

も同じことがいえます。その中には日本人が仏教を受け入れたインド人、16〜17世紀に日本に姿を見せたポルトガル人やスペイン人、オランダ人、そしてその後になって到来したアメリカ人やロシア人、フランス人やドイツ人が含まれます。

　日本人にとって外国語を身につけることがむずかしいという理由は、ひっくりかえせば、なぜ日本語が有力な国際語になりそうにないかを説明する役を果たします。日本語とその表記法は、外国人にとってとにかくむずかしすぎて習得できないのです。地域的な大言語というのはかなりの間にわたり存在してきましたが、国際語というのは比較的現代になってから出現した存在です。ローマ帝国時代を通じラテン語は地域言語でしたし、書きことばとしては最近まで、欧米の一部においてはその役割を維持しつづけてきました。漢文は東アジアの国際語としてラテン語よりずっと長いことその命脈を保ちました。アラビア語も、中近東の大部分、北アフリカ、それにヨーロッパの一部にとって、しばらくの間、同じ目的をつとめたのです。モンゴール語やトルコ語ですらが地域言語としての短い瞬間を歴史に留めました。スペイン語もある期間国際語になるのではという可能性を感じさせたものでした。

Spanish too gave promise for a while of becoming an international language.

French, however, may be the first language to have a valid claim to being a truly international language. Already widely used in trade in medieval times, it established itself as the leading tongue of Europe in the seventeenth and eighteenth centuries and continued as the language of diplomacy and culture into the nineteenth century in the West. But already in the eighteenth century, it was beginning to be replaced by English, which became clearly the international language of the nineteenth century. The supremacy of the British navy on the oceans of the world and England's wide conquests, including the absorption of all of India, were prime reasons for this development. But even more important than this was England's head start in industrialization and its resultant domination of trade.

This situation was reinforced almost unnoticed in the nineteenth century when the United States passed Great Britain as an industrial power and took a growing lead in world trade. Throughout the twentieth century, the increasing predominance of English as the world's

　でも、真の意味で国際語を称しうる最初のことばはフランス語ではなかったでしょうか。中世紀においてすらすでに通商で広く使われていたフランス語は、17〜18世紀に至り、主要なことばとしての地歩を確立し、19世紀に至るまで、欧米における外交と文化の唯一のことば、でありつづけました。しかし、すでに18世紀には、英語にとってかわられ始めました。そして19世紀には英語こそが明らかに国際語になったのです。7つの海を支配したイギリス海軍の優位、全インドを吸収した広範な世界支配、の2つがこの成り行きをもたらした主な理由でした。でもさらに重要だったのは、産業革命においてイギリスが先頭を切り、その結果として通商を支配したことにありました。

　この状況は19世紀に至り、アメリカ合衆国が工業力においてイギリスを追い抜き、世界通商における優位を高めるにともなって、ほとんどだれにも気づかれることなしに一層強化されたのです。20世紀を通じ、世界の最有力な国際語としての英語の圧倒的な優位はますます深まりましたが、それはイ

leading international language has depended more on America and comparable offshoots of England, such as Canada, Australia, and New Zealand, than on England itself.

The preponderant role of English as the world's chief international language seems destined to continue for some time into the future. It is the native language of the United States, the United Kingdom, and Canada—three of the world's seven largest industrial powers in the democratic first world. It is also the national language of many other smaller countries, including even the city-state of Singapore in which virtually all the citizens are not of English-speaking origin. It is the primary language for national political and economic affairs in countries like India and the Philippines. It is the undisputed second language for most of the other countries of the world, including even the Soviet Union and China. It would take tremendous upheavals in the world's economy and politics to unseat it from its present dominant position.

The replacement of English by Japanese as the world's chief international language is almost unimaginable despite Japan's great economic power today. One can hope

ギリス本国よりもむしろアメリカ合衆国、それにカナダ、オーストラリア、ニュージランドといった、合衆国と同じく本国から枝分かれした国々によるところが大きかったのです。

　世界の主要な国際語としての英語の圧倒的な役割は、これからもしばらくの間はひきつづくことが運命づけられているように見えます。英語はアメリカ合衆国、連合王国、それにカナダという、民主主義の上に立つ第一世界の7大工業国のうちの3つの母語なのです。英語はまたそれ以外の多くの小さな国々の国語でもあります。シンガポールはその一つです。この都市国家は、その人口のほとんどすべてが英語国系でないにもかかわらず、そうなのです。インドやフィリピンなどの国々では、英語は国家的な政治や経済に関する主要な言語ですし、それ以外のほとんどの国においては、第二言語としての地位は文句のつけようとてなく、その中にはソビエトや中国すらが含まれます。もし英語をいまの支配的な地位から引きずり降ろそうとすれば、世界経済や世界政治にたいへんな変動をもたらさずにはおかないでしょう。

　日本が巨大な経済力をもった今日とはいえ、主要国際語として日本語が英語にとってかわることは、ほとんど想像できません。もっと大勢の外国人が日本語をマスターする日がく

and expect that much larger numbers of foreigners will come to master Japanese in the future, but there are just too many hurdles standing in the way of its becoming a major international language to expect this to happen in the foreseeable future. The primary international language will undoubtedly continue to be English, and the Japanese, for the most part, will have to surmount the language problem from their side of the barrier.

Educational Reforms

How can this best be done? Because of the difficulties in pronunciation and the great differences in psychology and structure between Japanese and most other languages, it would be very helpful if the study of English could be started at a very early age—say at two or three, when the learning of foreign languages through songs and games is a pleasure, not a chore. One is continually hearing stories of Japanese businessmen and their wives in America being forced to fall back on their children of five or six to

ることを望み、それを期待することはできますが、有力な国際語の一つになるには、あまりにもそこに立ちはだかる障害がありすぎて、予見しうる将来においてはちょっと望み薄です。主要国際語が英語でありつづけるのは必至で、何としても日本人のほうから言語障壁を乗り越えるべく努力することが求められるでしょう。

教育改革

　ではそのためにはどうしたらいちばんよいのでしょうか。発音上の困難、それに日本語と他のほとんどのことばの間の心理面や構造面での違いからして、もしも英語学習が２、３歳という早期に始められたとすれば、おおいに役に立ちます。この年代ですと、唱歌やゲームを通じての外国語の習得は、楽しくはあっても、難行ではないからです。アメリカ合衆国にいる日本人ビズネスマンやその奥さんたちが、５つ６つの自分たちの子どもに通訳としておんぶせざるをえない、という話はしょっちゅう耳にします。家族ごと外国に住んでおれば、このような早期のスタートもらくなことはもちろんです。

serve as their interpreters. Such an early start is, of course easy when a Japanese family lives abroad, but it can also be achieved to some degree through good television programs and in playschool and kindergarten.

Even when the learning of a foreign language cannot be started at the preschool level, it would be desirable to push most school instruction in foreign languages down into the elementary years. English or any other foreign language can be learned at that age much more efficiently and with actual pleasure rather than pain. Such a change of curriculum would also open up considerable time in junior and senior high school for the study of more complex and advanced subjects.

I know that many Japanese are afraid that, if Japanese children are introduced to the study of foreign languages at too early an age, they will become confused in learning to speak or write Japanese correctly, but there is no reason for such worries. It is in fact a manifestation of Japanese isolationism. European children learn various foreign tongues at early ages with no impairment of their abilities in their own languages. Even small Dutch children often learn both English and German, two closely related lan-

しかし、これはよいテレビ番組それに保育園や幼稚園を通じてある程度までは達成可能です。

　就学前の段階で外国語学習ができないまでも、外国語の学校教育のほとんどを、小学校段階にまで年齢を引き下げることは望ましいでしょう。英語であれどんな外国語であれ、この年齢のほうが、より効率的に、しかも苦痛をともなわずに、心からの喜びとともに勉強できるのです。またこのようにカリキュラムを変えることで、中学校や高校では、もっと複雑で高度な科目を修めるための時間の捻出が可能となりましょう。

　もしも自分たちの子どもを、あまりにも初期に外国語の学習に向けさせたら、日本語を正しく話したり書いたりするうえに混乱がおきるのでは、と心配している日本人が少なくないことを、私は知っています。でも心配には及びません。のみならずそういう心配は、日本人の孤絶感のあらわれなのです。ヨーロッパの子どもはごく早期にいろいろな外国語を習いますが、別に自国語の能力が損なわれる、ということはありません。オランダではごくごく小さな子どもですらが、ドイツ語と英語という、オランダ語に近接した２つの外国語を習いますが、この３つのことばの間の差異をちゃんとわきま

guages to Dutch, while retaining the clear distinction between the three and their complete mastery of their own native tongue. Japanese who speak so different a language from most other people and have a unique writing system should suffer no confusion whatsoever between Japanese and English or any other foreign language.

Unfortunately all of you are too old to recommence your beginnings in language learning; and, in any case, this is the sort of thing decided by one's parents, not by small children. In planning for the next generation, however, such innovations should be borne in mind.

Even if English teaching in Japan continues to be concentrated in junior and senior high schools, many improvements should be made. It is doubtful that any other country uses so much formal school time for the learning of English with such meager results as in the case in Japan. A major problem is that few Japanese teachers of English have adequate skills themselves in the pronunciation and speaking of English. The use of katakana to transcribe English words and names only confirms Japanese in their mispronunciations.

え、しかも母語のオランダ語は完璧にマスターしているのです。日本人は、ほとんどの外国人とはまったくちがったことばを話し、しかも独特な表記法をもっているわけですから、日本語と、英語ないしは他の外国語とがこんがらがってしまう、というようなことは絶対にありえないはずです。

　残念ながら皆さん方にとっては、言語学習をはじめからやり直すことなど、年齢的に無理ですし、いずれにせよ、これは子どもたち自身ではなく、両親が決めることです。ただ次の世代のために備えるにあたっては、このような改革案も考慮されてしかるべきでしょう。

　日本の英語教育がこれからも中・高に集中しつづけるとしても、多くの改善がなされる必要があります。学校教育の中で英語の予習にこれほど多くの正規の授業時間をあてながら、これほど貧寒な結果しか手にしていない国が他にはたしてあるだろうかと、疑わしくなるくらいです。一つの大きな問題は、日本の英語教師自身が英語の発音や話し方という面で、十分な技量を持ち合わせない、という点です。英語の単語や名前の片仮名による表記も、まちがい発音を定着させるだけです。

Another major problem is that most English instruction in Japanese schools is aimed at the wrong goals. Very little time is devoted to acquiring the ability to understand English by ear and expressing oneself in understandable speech. The chief emphasis is placed on grammatical analysis, usually presented in Japanese, and in attempting to learn to read difficult classical texts, which are of much less value to the student than is practical everyday spoken English. Even native English speakers would find the grammatical instruction confusing as well as unnecessary, and the classical texts are even to them difficult and boring. Worst of all, classroom instruction in English in Japan focuses on preparing students to pass impractical entrance examinations to higher levels of education, rather than on learning to comprehend, speak, and read ordinary contemporary English. The learning of English is not seen as the acquisition of an exciting new skill but as one of the least pleasant aspects of the so-called examination hell. Most of a student's original enthusiasm for learning something new and useful is smothered from the start.

No one need be surprised by the poor results of English education in Japan. The whole system is in bad need

　いま一つの大きな問題点は、日本の学校における英語教授
が、まちがった目標に向けられているということです。耳で
英語を聞きとる能力の習得や、なんとかわかってもらえるよ
うな形での自己表現には、ほんの少しの時間しか向けられて
いないのです。主な力点は文法的な分析——それも日本語で
なされることがほとんどです——と、学生にとっては日常実
用の話しことばよりははるかに価値の低い、小むずかしい古
典の文章をなんとか読めるようになることに置かれています。
英語を母語とする者にとってすら、文法についての講釈など
不必要なばかりか頭がこんがらがるだけでしょうし、古典に
至っては、むずかしくて退くつなだけでしょう。いちばん悪
いことは日本の学校における英語教育は、上級学校への役立
たずの入学試験に合格するための準備に集中して、ふつうの
現代英語を理解し話し読むことを身につけようとさせてない
ことです。英語を習うということは、わくわくするような新
しい技能を身につけることではなくて、いわゆる受験地獄の
中でもいちばん愉快でない側面の一つとみなされているので
す。生徒がもともともっていた、なにか役に立つ新しいもの
を習いたいという熱意の大半は、のっけからめったうちにさ
れるのです。

　日本の英語教育が貧しい成果しか生み出していないことは、
なにも驚くにはあたりません。制度全体が改革をひどく必要

of revision. Japan has the money and facilities to do this. It can afford to hire large numbers of native speakers of English, though care should be taken to select only those with special training and experience in the teaching of English as a foreign language. Language laboratories with good electronic equipment can assist students in learning to understand English by ear and in speaking it with an understandable pronunciation and reasonable accuracy.

The whole English curriculum and the methods of instruction call out for thorough revision. To many Japanese, this may seem a minor matter, but it is of vital importance if Japan, in its own interests, is to play the international role it should and individual Japanese are to develop the sense of being citizens of the world that is required of them at this stage in history.

What You Can Do Now

Such educational reforms may suffice for the next generation if they are made in time, but what should you

としているのです。日本にはそのためのお金もあれば施設も
あります。また、外国語としての英語教育について専門の訓
練や経験をもった人だけを選ぶという注意を払ったうえで、
多数の英語国人を雇うこともできます。よい電子機器を備え
たＬＬの設備をつかえば、生徒が英語を耳から理解し、理
解可能な発音と相当程度の正確さで話すことを身につけるう
えの助けになります。英語のカリキュラムのすべてと教授法
には、徹底的な改革が必要です。日本人の多くにしてみれば、
そんなことはたいしたことでないように見えるかもしれませ
んが、もしも日本が、自己利益のために、当然すべき国際的
な役割を果たし、一人一人の日本人が、歴史の現段階におい
て要求されている世界市民としての意識を作り出していこう
とするなら、これは日本にとり決定的な重要性をもつことが
らなのです。

あなたにいまできること

　このような教育改革は、もし間に合うように手がけられれ
ば、次の世代にとっては十分なものかもしれません。でも、

143

young Japanese do who have already completed all or most of your formal education? This is basically a matter of your own will power. There is much that you can do on your own. What is required is for you to understand the importance of the problem and devote the necessary time and effort to it. There are various good approaches to the learning of English, and you should adopt the one or the combination of approaches which best fits your situation. The important thing is that you should pursue your studies seriously, devoting an appreciable amount of time and effort to them on a regular basis, daily if at all possible.

There are many tutors of English in Japan and also English teaching juku, which is perhaps best translated by the vague term of "academy." Unfortunately many of the tutors and juku are not very good, so special care should be taken in choosing between them. You can also do a great deal without such formal aid. Between the radio, video, and various other electronic aids, you can develop your ability to comprehend English by ear and even improve your speech to some extent.

As I have also pointed out previously in other con-

すでに学校教育のすべてもしくはほとんどを済ませてしまった若い日本人は、いったい何をすべきなのでしょうか。これは何といってもまず一人一人の意志力の問題です。自分たちでできることは、うんとあるのです。皆さんに求められるのは問題の重要性を理解し、そのために必要な時間を割き努力することです。英語の習得にはいろいろなすぐれた方法がありますが、皆さんとしては自分の状況に見合った方法を、単独もしくはいくつかの組み合わせで選びとっていくべきです。大事なのは真剣にとりくんでいくことで、それを規則的に、できたら毎日、相当量の時間と努力を向けることです。

日本には英語の個人教師も数多く、英語では academy という漠然としたことばで呼ぶしかない「塾」なるものもたくさんあります。不幸なことにその多くはたいしたことがないので、よほど注意して選択することが大切です。このような正規の助けなしでも成果をあげることは可能です。ラジオやビデオ、ほかにも電子関係の補助教材を使いわけることで、耳から聞いて英語を理解する能力を身につけることができるほか、ある程度までは話す力を改善向上することも可能です。

他のテーマとの関連ですでに指摘したように、英語を（母

texts, you should use every opportunity you have to develop contacts with English-speaking persons and spend as much time as you can in conversation with them. You should be willing to make mistakes and try to persuade some native speaker of English to correct you whenever possible. Competence in understanding and speaking any language comes from using it. Classroom study is at best just a poor substitute for that. You should pass up no chance to listen to spoken English, whether it be in one of the several American and Canadian accents, Australian, or one of the various pronunciations of the British Isles. Then you should speak out freely as best you can. Don't be afraid to make mistakes and don't worry too much about specific accents. Unless you are a very advanced speaker of English, it will not be at all evident to a native speaker what specific English accent you may be trying to imitate.

I am reminded of my own experience when I was a graduate student in France some 55 years ago and did my best to master both French and German. My fiancée, who later became my wife for 20 years until her death in 1955, happened to be a graduate student in Austria. Since both of us were native speakers of English, that was of course

語として）話す人々とのかかわりを深める機会はこれを一つ
残らず利用し、できるだけ多くの時間を費してその人々と話
し合うよう努めなければなりません。間違いをおかすことに
ビクビクせず、英語を母語とする人にできうるかぎり直して
くれるよう説得しなければなりません。どんなことばであれ、
それを理解し話すうえでの高い能力は、実地に使うことによ
って得られます。教室内での勉強は、よくてもせいぜいが実
地に使用することのおそまつな代替物でしかありません。英
語の話しことばを耳にする機会があれば、それをのがしては
なりません。合衆国もしくはカナダ式のいくつかの話し方の
一つであろうと、オーストラリア式であろうと、ブリテン島
のいくつもある発音の一つであろうと、それは問うところで
はありません。またできるだけ自由に思っていることを口に
出すべきです。間違いをすることを恐れてはなりませんし、
英語といっても特定の訛りについて気に病むこともありませ
ん。あなたが話す英語がよほど高レベルでもないかぎり、あ
なたがいくつもある英語の訛りのうち、どれを身につけよう
と思っているのかは、ネイティブ・スピーカーにとって明白
ではありえないからです。

　55年もの昔に、私がフランスで大学院生だったときの個人
的な体験を思いおこします。フランス語とドイツ語の両方を
マスターしようと思っていた頃のことです。私のフィアンセ
──その後1955年に亡くなるまで20年間も私の妻であった人
ですが──もたまたまオーストリアで勉強中の大学院生でし

our chief language of communication, but in order to maximize our use of French and German, we wrote all our love letters to each other in German and French, she in German and I in French. We also frequently spoke French or German together, depending on the place in Europe where we happened to be. I found that in simple conversations I was quickly accepted by German speakers as being a speaker of some outlandish German dialect, and I was elated after a year in France to be no longer identified as a native speaker of English but perhaps as a Pole or German. Not many people will have the chance to repeat my experience, but I do know several Japanese couples temporarily in the United States who speak together in English as much as they can, and I have noticed how quickly their English improves in comparison with some other less adventuresome Japanese I know.

This raises one important related point. You must be brave in daring to use your English as much as you can. Japanese tend to be somewhat reticent even in speaking Japanese, and they are downright timid in speaking foreign languages. This is a deeply ingrained cultural trait. But you will find that good language learners are usually

た。2人とも英語を母語としていましたから、意思疎通にあたっては主として英語を使ったことはいうまでもありませんが、フランス語とドイツ語とを最大限に使うためにお互いのラブレターはドイツ語とフランス語で書くことにしたのです。私はたまたまヨーロッパのどこに居合わせたかによってしばしば彼女あてにフランス語で、彼女は私にあててドイツ語で、というわけです。また2人はフランス語もしくはドイツ語で話したものです。簡単な会話ですと、私はドイツ人から、どこかへんぴなドイツ語方言の話し手として受け入れられるようになりました。また1年間をフランスで過ごしたあとのこと、私の母語が英語ではなく、ポーランド人かドイツ人とみなされるようになったときには、うんと喜んだものです。私のような経験はだれにでも追体験できるものではありません。でも一時的にアメリカにいる日本人で、できるだけお互いに英語で話し合うことにしているカップルを何組も知っていますし、それ以外の引っ込み思案の日本人と比べて、この人たちの英語力の向上がいかに迅速か、気づいてもいます。

　ここで一つ関連する重要な点が出てきます。できるだけ英語を使うという点で、大胆でなければならないということです。日本人はややもすると日本語を使うにあたってもどちらかというと寡黙です。そして外国語を話すという段になると臆病もいいところです。これは深いところに根ざした文化的な性向です。でもことばのよい学習者というのは、まだその

149

people who are willing to try to speak out in foreign languages even when their skills are still not highly developed. Just as in learning to become world citizens, Japanese must go against their natural social tendencies and force themselves to speak out even in clumsy English. The only way to learn to speak a foreign language is by speaking it. No Japanese baby starts by speaking perfect Japanese. Similarly no Japanese young person or adult can expect to start out by speaking perfect English.

In discussing the internationalization of Japan, I have stressed three main interrelated points. You young Japanese need to know more about the rest of the world and also about Japan itself. You need to understand how Japan is part of an interdependent world and learn to feel yourselves to be world citizens. And you need to be able to communicate with the other peoples of the world. These are large undertakings, but I believe that you can achieve them in large part on your own if you really devote yourself to the effort. Your personal future and that of Japan and the world as a whole depend on how well you succeed in mastering these tasks.

外国語の技能が十分でもないのに、平気で話す人に多いということに気づくことでしょう。世界市民を目指して努力するのと同様に、日本人は生まれついての社会的な傾向にさからっても、たとえたどたどしくあろうと、英語で話すよう自分自身に強制すべきです。外国語が話せるようになる唯一の道は、話してみることだからです。日本人の赤ん坊だって、はじめからチャンとした日本語が話せるわけではありません。同様に、日本人の若者や成人がはじめから完全な英語が話せるなんて、そんなことは望むべくもないのです。

　日本の国際化を論ずるにあたり、私は3つの関連するポイントに重点をおきました。皆さん方日本の若者は、世界のこと、そして日本自身のことをもっと知らなければなりません。また日本がどのように相互依存度の高い世界の一部であるかを理解し、世界市民という意識をもつことができるよう学んでいかなければなりません。そして世界の他の諸民族と意思疎通ができるようになる必要があります。これらはいずれも大きな課題です。でも皆さんがそのために本気で献身すれば、ほとんど自前で達成できることばかりだと私は信じています。皆さん一人一人の未来や日本の将来、そして世界全体の将来は、これらの課題を皆さんがどううまくこなしていくかにかかっているのです。

訳者あとがき

　国際化とか国際的、というのはいまや日本でいちばんよく使われる、しかもプラスのイメージをともなったことばといえるでしょう。ためしに身近な電話帳を引いて、国際うんぬんという名前の会社や組織がどれほど多いかをたしかめてみてください。きっとその多さにびっくりするでしょう。

　事実、国際うんぬんということばは、アメリカ人にとってのmotherhoodとかthe flag, Godとかapple pieということばと同じくらいの倫理的な光背というか後光を背中にしょっているのです。

　ただそれだけにこのことば、ライシャワーさんもいうように流行語化してしまい、それがいったい何を意味するのか、また日本人にとってそれがどのような機会とともに制約をもたらすのか、つまりはプラスとともにどのようなマイナスをともなうのかについての吟味は、決して十分とはいえません。にもかかわらず、国際化ばかりは着実に進行していきます。

　しかも恐ろしいのは、国際化の進行や深化にともない、さまざまな問題や困難が表面化するにつれ、下手をすると、国粋化というか、一種のxenophobia的な傾向がじわじわと立ちのぼってくることです。際と粋とは、たった1音のちが

いですが、この両者の差異は深刻かつ重大です。

　世界の中の日本、という立場をたとえ苦しくても息永く貫いていかぬかぎり、日本や日本人、とくに若い皆さんの、未来なぞありえません。この地球というホシはますます小さなところになる一方です。ライシャワーさんのいう shrink-age of space（空間の圧縮）、トインビー博士のいう annihilation of distance（距離の破壊）は、それこそ目くるめくほどの速度で進んでいます。あと20年かそこいらで、東京・パリは２時間ちょっとの、東京・サンフランシスコは１時間少々の飛行時間に収まるといいます。

　そして、日本の企業は販売拠点や流通拠点だけでなく、生産拠点や研究開発拠点ですら、どんどん海外に移していくでしょうし、それとともにヒトもまた日本を後にしなければならなくなります。

　逆に外国人労働者や外国人花嫁が社会問題化し、行政や政治の舞台にのせられている昨今の傾向は、もっと深まっていくにちがいありません。われわれ自身が外に出ていくだけでなく、日本のお互いの身の回りに外国人がいまよりもさらに濃密な形で存在するようになるのは必至です。

　国際化ということをわれわれ庶民の、とくに若い皆さんの身の丈や目線で考えると、こういう意味合いをもつのです。皆さんの大学や高校でも外国人の教官や留学生の数が、もっとふえていくでしょうし、またそれが必要でしょう。

　ライシャワーさんは、つとにこういう点を説いてきました。欧米における日本研究の第一人者として、日本と日本人に対する愛情の深さに催され、国際化という立場からする日本のあやうげさを折にふれて指摘し、その実情の認識と、事態の改善の必要を訴えつづけてきました。その『ザ・ジャパニーズ』や『ライシャワーの日本史』——いずれも小生の訳書が文藝春秋から出ています——の中に、ライシャワーさんの切実な声を読みとることができます。

　この本はライシャワーさんが、とくに日本の若い皆さんを対象に、以上のような問題意識と懸念とを、率直かつ自在に述べたものです。率直さはライシャワーさんの、皆さんと日本の未来への思い入れの深さのあらわれと捉えるべきでしょう。

　翻訳にあたっては、対訳ということもあり、『ザ・ジャパニーズ』や『ライシャワーの日本史』のときとは違って、意

訳よりは直訳に近づけました。ライシャワーさんも私も、直訳を好まないほうなのですが、この本の性格上、むしろ直訳風の訳文をしたためました。ご理解をいただきたく思います。

　なお、チャールズ・イー・タトル出版の米山幸伸さんには編集その他の面でお世話になりました。お礼申します。また、中央大学商学部の出身でいまはアメリカの州立モンタナ大学大学院にある松田良明君が、とかく自由訳に向かいがちで、しかも漢語や擬古調に赴きがちな小生の訳文を、原文からあまり逸脱せず、ヤングにも受け入れられるようないまの日本語へと、たづなを引きしめてくれた友情にもお礼を述べるものです。

國弘 正雄

著者略歴 （編集部製作）

1910	10月15日　父オーガスト・カール、母ヘレン・オールドファーザーの二男として明治学院内宣教師館で生まれる。
1916	日本アメリカンスクールに入学。
1918	父オーガスト、新渡戸稲造、安井てつらの協力を得て、東京女子大学を創立。
1927	日本アメリカンスクール卒業。 オーバリン大学に入学。
1931	オーバリン大学卒業後、ハーバード大学大学院歴史学部に入学。
1932	ハーバード大学修士（MA）
1933	ハーバード燕京研究所のフェロー奨学金にて、パリ大学へ留学。 ヨーロッパ各地を旅行。
1935	シベリア横断鉄道にて8年ぶりに日本を訪れ、すでに日本の女学校で英語を教えていたアドリエン・ダントンと東京で結婚。

1937	ライシャワー夫妻、円仁研究のため朝鮮を訪れ、ついで北京へ行く。
1938	アメリカへ帰リ、ハーバード燕京研究所で博士論文執筆。
1939	円仁研究により博士号 (Ph. D) を取得。 エリセーエフと共同で日本語の講座を始める。
1941	国務省極東課に一時勤務。
1942	陸軍通信隊の依頼でワシントンに赴き、翻訳者と暗号解読者を養成する学校の組織と運営に従事。
1943	陸軍参謀部 G II の要請により少佐に任官。日本軍発信の暗号電報の情報を分析。後に中佐に昇進。
1945	国務省極東部長の特別補佐官として入省。
1946	ハーバード大学に戻リ、再び学究生活に入る。
1950	ハーバード大学極東言語学部の正教授に昇進。
1952	マサチューセッツ州ベルモントへ移転。

1955	妻アドリエン長年患ってきた心臓病のため死去。ハーバード燕京研究所の次期所長に内定したので、3人の子どもとともに日本へ行き、ついで東アジア各地を訪れる。
1956	前年知り合った松方ハルと東京にて再婚。(松方ハルは、明治の元勲松方正義の孫娘で、アメリカンスクール卒業後、米国ブリンシピア大学へ留学。第二次大戦後、外国誌記者として活躍、外人記者クラブ初の日本人会員、初の女性役員となる。著書に『絹と武士』がある。)
1957	オーバリン大学より名誉博士号を授与される。
1960	ハーバード燕京研究所長として、東アジア各地へ出張。
1961	ケネディ政権の下、第17代駐日大使に任命され、日本に赴任。
1964	精神障害の青年に包丁で腿を刺され3週間入院。退院後、ハワイで療養。しかし、陸軍病院に再入院、以後2ケ月近い入院生活を送る。

1966 駐日大使の職を辞して離日、ハーバード大学へ戻る。
　　　 ハーバード大学より名誉あるユニバーシティ・プロ
　　　 フェッサーという自由なポストに任命される。

1967 「たんぼ講座」を再開。日米関係の緊密化を反映し、
　　　 ハーバード大学の人気講座となる。

1975 日本学士院の客員に指名される。
　　　 国際交流基金賞を授与される。

1977 ハーバード大学出版会より『ザ・ジャパニーズ』が
　　　 出版され、日米両国でベストセラーとなる。

1981 ハーバード大学を定年退職。

1983 ハーバード燕京研究所の理事長を辞す。